the PURITY PRINCIPLE

RANDY ALCORN

Learning Activities and Leader Guide
by Debbie Kubik Evert

LifeWay Press®
Nashville, Tennessee

ISBN 1-4158-2014-7

This book is a resource for course CG-1066 in the Personal Life category of the Christian Growth Study Plan.

Dewey Decimal Classification: 176
Subject Headings: SEXUAL ABSTINENCE \ SEXUAL BEHAVIOR

Photography:
Volvox, PictureQuest
Inset: Michael Gomez

Unless otherwise noted, all Scripture quotations are taken from the Holman Christian Standard Bible®, copyright © 1999, 2000, 2001, 2002, 2003 by Holman Bible Publishers. Used by permission.

Scripture quotations identified NIV are from the Holy Bible, New International Version, copyright © 1973, 1978, 1984 by International Bible Society. Used by permission.

The Scripture quotation identified NASB is taken from the NEW AMERICAN STANDARD BIBLE, © Copyright 1960, 1962, 1963, 1968, 1971, 1972, 1973, 1975, 1977, 1995. Used by permission.

Scripture quotations identified Phillips are reprinted with permission of Macmillan Publishing Co., Inc., from J. B. Phillips: The New Testament in Modern English, Revised Edition. © J. B. Phillips 1958, 1960, 1972.

To order additional copies of this resource: WRITE to LifeWay Church Resources Customer Service; One LifeWay Plaza; Nashville, TN 37234-0113; FAX (615) 251-5933; PHONE toll free (800) 458-2772; E-MAIL *customerservice@lifeway.com;* ORDER ONLINE at *www.lifeway.com;* or VISIT the LifeWay Christian Store serving you.

Printed in the United States of America

Leadership and Adult Publishing
LifeWay Church Resources
One LifeWay Plaza
Nashville, TN 37234-0175

Contents

About the Author

Randy Alcorn, a former pastor and a best-selling author, is the founder and director of Eternal Perspective Ministries (EPM), a nonprofit organization dedicated to teaching biblical truth and drawing attention to the needy. EPM exists to meet the needs of the unreached, unfed, unborn, uneducated, unreconciled, and unsupported people around the world. "My ministry focus is communicating the strategic importance of using our earthly time, money, possessions, and opportunities to invest in need-meeting ministries that count for eternity," Alcorn says. "I do that by trying to analyze, teach, and apply the implications of Christian truth."

Alcorn's novels include *Deadline, Dominion, Edge of Eternity, Lord Foulgrin's Letters, The Ishbane Conspiracy,* and *Safely Home.* His nonfiction books include *The Treasure Principle; The Grace and Truth Paradox; In Light of Eternity; ProLife Answers to ProChoice Arguments; Money, Possessions, and Eternity;* and *Heaven.*

Alcorn attended Multnomah Bible College and Western Seminary, where he received his bachelor of theology, master of arts in biblical studies, and doctor of divinity. He and his wife, Nanci, live in Gresham, Oregon, and have two married daughters, Karina Franklin and Angela Stump.

Preface

Of all God's gifts to humanity, none holds greater potential for abuse than sex. Designed to bring us intimacy and happiness, sex has the power, when mishandled, to destroy relationships and produce intense suffering. Consequently, our permissive society is littered with the refuse of lives shattered by sexual abuse, pornography, sexual addiction, molestation, adultery, sexually transmitted diseases, and emotional devastation.

God never intended it to be this way. He expects His children to live a life of purity, a plan that is designed not only for His glory but also for our benefit. Obedience sets us on the path to a higher pleasure—a life that brings us incomparable joy, pleases our loving Father, and yields eternal rewards.

This study vividly portrays the choices that each individual must make between purity and impurity—and the serious consequences of those choices. By understanding God's ideal for a life of purity, you will see impurity as idolatry that offends God and keeps you from gaining the best He offers you. From Scripture you will learn why the Purity Principle is true: that purity is always smart and impurity is always stupid. Because the battle for purity takes place in the mind, you will adopt biblical strategies that fortify your mind to fight sexual temptation, and you will learn practical guidelines for living a life of purity, whether you are married or single.

Purity is always smart. Impurity is always stupid. The choice is yours. This study will help you make smart choices.

week 1

God's Plan for Sexual Purity

day 1

Smart or Stupid?

Lucinda, a Christian, decided that her husband wasn't romantic enough. A decent, hardworking, churchgoing guy, he just didn't live up to the Prince Charming images of Hollywood. So Lucinda became involved with another man, eventually marrying him. Years later, after bringing unspeakable grief to her family and herself, she came back to Christ. "I wish I had my first husband back," she admitted. "But now it's too late." God has forgiven Lucinda and still has plans for her. Yet she has paid a fearful price. Lucinda has forfeited what was hers—and what could have been hers.

Name some blessings Lucinda forfeited by her decision.

_____

_____

Lucinda gave up a clear conscience and a priceless sense of peace; warm, satisfying years of companionship; the respect and affection of children and grandchildren; a ministry touching many lives; or rewards—exceeding all imagination—in the life to come. Yes, God has forgiven Lucinda, but the consequences of her choices remain. She still lives with the realization that she could have had so much more if she had followed God's plan for sexual purity.

What do you think is meant by the term *sexual purity*?

_____

Sexual purity is an absolute commitment of your sexual needs, desires, thoughts, and actions to God. For a single person, that commitment includes abstaining from sexual intercourse until marriage. For married people like Lucinda, it means being completely faithful to your spouse in your thoughts and actions.

Sadly, Lucinda thought she was acting in her own best interest when she followed her lust. If we could have obtained an honest interview with her just before she trashed her purity, she would have said: "This is for me. This is for my happiness." Yet it wasn't. Not even close. It never is. Without intending to, Lucinda acted against her own self-interest. What she did wasn't just wrong. It was stupid.

Since the time we were young teenagers, many of us have been told to remain sexually pure, and we were probably given a variety of reasons. The bottom line is: God commands purity and forbids impurity. Purity is right. Impurity is wrong.

Look at what God has to say about sexual purity and impurity. Match the Scripture reference with the truth found in it.

____ 1. Exodus 20:14 a. Flee from sexual immorality.

____ 2. Acts 15:20   b. Keep yourself pure.

____ 3. 1 Corinthians 6:18 c. God has not called us to
           impurity but to sanctification.

____ 4. Colossians 3:5 d. Do not commit adultery.

____ 5. 1 Thessalonians 4:7 e. Put to death whatever in you
           is worldly.

____ 6. 1 Timothy 5:22 f. Abstain from sexual
           immorality.

7

As these verses teach, God's position is that purity is always smart; impurity is always stupid. That's what I call the Purity Principle: purity is always smart; impurity is always stupid. Not sometimes. Not usually. Always. You're not an exception. I'm not an exception. There are no exceptions.

In this study we are going to learn why the Purity Principle is true—why it is always smart to follow God's design for purity and why it is always stupid to do otherwise. You might be thinking: *That's not so profound. I'm a Christian, and I know the difference between right and wrong.* But surveys indicate that the sexual morality of today's Christians has become almost indistinguishable from that of non-Christians. It's often impossible to discern where the world ends and the church begins.

Check each statement that is true for believers who live in a sex-saturated culture.

❏ It's OK for us to adopt the sexually permissive habits of our culture.
❏ It's easy for us to adopt the impure lifestyle of our culture.
❏ We will eventually give in to sexual temptation.
❏ We must fight hard to maintain a lifestyle of purity.

Being a believer in a culture that constantly bombards us with sexual messages doesn't mean that believers are destined to succumb to sexual temptation. It means that it's easy for us to adopt attitudes and thought patterns that could lead to immoral, ungodly choices. We must make a concerted effort to reject these influences and to choose the life of purity that God wants for us.

Our failure in the area of purity has devastating consequences, not only for our personal lives and the lives of our families but also for the church as a whole. Why? Because if believers are just like the world, we have nothing to offer it. An unholy church will never win an unholy world to Christ.

Why is sexual purity such an integral part of a rewarding life? Why is premarital and extramarital sex so toxic to joy?

Why have so many tried and tried and tried—yet failed and failed and failed? How can we avoid the lures and snares that lock us into bondage and tear away the abundant life? These questions—and others like them—have been discussed for years. God has graciously given us examples in His Word of those who did—and didn't—fare so well.

Assess your attitude toward purity as you begin this study.
❏ I want to learn God's teachings on purity and live a pure life that pleases Him.
❏ I'm not convinced the issue of purity is very important.

It's no overstatement to call this a life-and-death issue. The time you take to complete the rest of this study could save you from disaster. It could set you on a course for which you—and your family—will always be grateful.

THE DAY IN REVIEW

Review today's lesson.
What was the most important concept you read today?

_____

_____

How will this truth challenge you to be like Christ?

_____

_____

Think about any stupid decisions you have made, thinking that you were acting in your best interest. Ask God to use this study to teach you His standards for purity. Write your prayer below.

_____

_____

_____

_____

Pursuing God's Ideal

day 2

Tiffany and Kyle grew up in church. When the youth pastor warned against premarital sex, they had trouble taking him seriously. After all, everything in their culture—movies, television, and music—focused on sex. One night after their youth group, Tiffany gave in to Kyle. It was painful and nauseating—nothing like in the movies. Afterward she felt horrible. Kyle was mad at her because she wasn't supposed to let it happen.

Tiffany started sleeping around, trying to find a guy who would love her. She never did. Men used her and moved on. She quit going to church. One day she discovered that she was pregnant. A friend drove her to an abortion clinic. Now she is plagued by dreams about the child she killed.

Tiffany could turn to Christ. He would forgive her. But her heart is so broken and calloused now that she doesn't believe that forgiveness is possible. She has attempted suicide. A street prostitute, she is on drugs and has been raped. Recently she had another abortion. Her eyes are dead. So is her hope.

Kyle? He's lost interest in spiritual things. He's at college now, an atheist. He's had sex with several girls. Feeling empty, he experiments with anything he thinks might bring him happiness.

Fill in the blanks.

Tiffany and Kyle wanted sexual excitement but got _____.
Their belief in God turned to _____.
Tiffany's desire for intimacy resulted in _____.
Kyle wanted happiness but got _____.

It didn't have to be this way. The pain, the disbelief, the misery, the emptiness, the hopelessness—this isn't what God wants for us. He wants the very best for His children:

BLESSED BE THE GOD AND FATHER OF OUR LORD JESUS CHRIST, WHO HAS BLESSED US WITH EVERY SPIRITUAL BLESSING IN THE HEAVENS, IN CHRIST; FOR HE CHOSE US IN HIM, BEFORE THE FOUNDATION OF THE WORLD, TO BE HOLY AND BLAMELESS IN HIS SIGHT. IN LOVE HE PREDESTINED US TO BE ADOPTED THROUGH JESUS CHRIST FOR HIMSELF, ACCORDING TO HIS FAVOR AND WILL, TO THE PRAISE OF HIS GLORIOUS GRACE THAT HE FAVORED US WITH IN THE BELOVED. *EPHESIANS 1:3-6*

If we are God's adopted children through Christ, then all of those blessings are ours.

Those verses express an amazing thing: through the blood of Jesus, God sees us as "holy and blameless" (v. 4). The word *holy* means *separated* or *set apart*. God's holiness means that He is morally superior to humans. When referring to Christians, *holiness* means that God has set us apart for His purposes and service. Because God is holy, He wants us to be holy, and He expects us to live pure and holy lives:

AS THE ONE WHO CALLED YOU IS HOLY, YOU ALSO ARE TO BE HOLY IN ALL YOUR CONDUCT; FOR IT IS WRITTEN, BE HOLY, BECAUSE I AM HOLY. *1 PETER 1:15-16*

A major reason purity is always smart is that God's children can be happy only when we mirror His character and conform to His standards for living. He made us to enjoy a love relationship with Him for all eternity. Nothing else satisfies.

Love for God is a great motivation for honoring His standards for a holy, pure life. In the Old Testament as God was establishing His covenant with His people, He reminded them that obedience was an essential part of loving Him. To love God was to obey Him; to obey God was to love Him:

LOVE THE LORD YOUR GOD AND ALWAYS KEEP HIS MANDATE AND HIS STATUTES, ORDINANCES, AND COMMANDS. *DEUTERONOMY 11:1*

Jesus also connected obeying and loving God:

LOVE THE LORD YOUR GOD WITH ALL YOUR HEART, WITH ALL YOUR SOUL, AND WITH ALL YOUR MIND. *MATTHEW 22:37*

IF YOU LOVE ME, YOU WILL KEEP MY COMMANDMENTS. *JOHN 14:15*

If we love God, we obey His commandments about godly living.

Do you love God so much that you want to obey Him?
❏ Yes   ❏ No

Another motivation for honoring God's design for purity is fear. Moses asked,

WHAT DOES THE LORD YOUR GOD ASK OF YOU EXCEPT TO FEAR THE LORD YOUR GOD BY WALKING IN ALL HIS WAYS, TO LOVE HIM [THERE'S THAT LOVE COMMAND AGAIN], AND TO WORSHIP THE LORD YOUR GOD WITH ALL YOUR HEART AND ALL YOUR SOUL? *DEUTERONOMY 10:12*

Rephrase in your own words the expression "to fear the Lord your God by walking in all His ways."

_____

This phrase means that you give God the reverence He deserves by obeying Him. To fear God is to have a profound respect for His holiness—and for the consequences of disobeying Him. Weighing these consequences can motivate us to purity.

Check potential consequences of sexual impurity.

❏ Becoming a sexual predator   ❏ Molesting others
❏ Always feeling loved   ❏ Being sent to prison
❏ Acquiring a disease   ❏ Gaining respect
❏ Destroying relationships   ❏ Being trustworthy

Would any of these consequences strike enough fear in you not to disobey God? ❏ Yes ❏ No

The fear of God shouldn't scare us out of our wits; it should scare us into them:

THE FEAR OF THE LORD IS A FOUNTAIN OF LIFE,
TURNING PEOPLE FROM THE SNARES OF DEATH. *PROVERBS 14:27*

Another reason believers want to pursue God's ideal for sexual purity is God's promise to reward a life of obedience to Him. When I talk about rewards, I'm not talking about eternal life or heaven. If you have accepted Christ, your faith in Him has already determined your eternal destination. But your behavior determines the eternal rewards you will receive. Read what the writer of Hebrews said about faith and rewards:

WITHOUT FAITH IT IS IMPOSSIBLE TO PLEASE GOD, FOR THE ONE WHO DRAWS NEAR TO HIM MUST BELIEVE THAT HE EXISTS AND REWARDS THOSE WHO SEEK HIM. *HEBREWS 11:6*

God will surely reward us for making choices that please Him. Obedience to His will and His way forms the underlying lattice for that rarest and most wonderful human condition—joy.

    Like Tiffany and Kyle, we all face the choice of obedience or disobedience, and we all reap the consequences of that choice. When Cain, humanity's firstborn, stood at a moral crossroads, God gently reasoned with him:

WHY ARE YOU FURIOUS? AND WHY ARE YOU DOWNCAST? IF YOU DO RIGHT, WON'T YOU BE ACCEPTED? BUT IF YOU DO NOT DO RIGHT, SIN IS CROUCHING AT THE DOOR. ITS DESIRE IS FOR YOU, BUT YOU MUST MASTER IT. *GENESIS 4:6-7*

God was saying: "If you choose My plan, you'll find happiness. If you say no to the sinful desires that want to master you, if you walk with Me, you'll experience My peace. If you reject My standards, you surrender to forces that will tear your life apart."

Cain chose unwisely. The rest is history.

THE DAY IN REVIEW

Review today's lesson.
What was the most important concept you read today?

_____

How will this truth challenge you to be like Christ?

_____

Praise God for His holiness and express your desire to live a holy life. Express your love for Him and your fear of Him— your reverence and awe. Thank Him for the eternal rewards He has promised for obedience. Write your prayer below.

_____

_____

_____

_____

_____

Worthless Idols

day **3**

An idol is something more than a grotesque statue with big lips and a ruby in its navel. It's a God-substitute. It's something—anything—we value more highly than God. When we cling to an idol, we always make a trade: something else for God.

The prophet Jonah, inside the digestive tract of a great fish beneath the Mediterranean Sea, made this observation:

THOSE WHO CLING TO WORTHLESS IDOLS
FORFEIT THE GRACE THAT COULD BE THEIRS. *JONAH 2:8, NIV*

Sexual sin is idolatry because it puts our desires in the place of God. Our sexual behavior reveals who or what rules our lives.

Paul the apostle addressed this issue in his letter to the church in Rome. Sadly, from the beginning of time, people have rejected God and have chosen God-substitutes.

**In the following verses circle the words
that identify people's state of mind.
Underline the actions that resulted from their thinking.**

THOUGH THEY KNEW GOD, THEY DID NOT GLORIFY HIM AS GOD OR SHOW GRATITUDE. INSTEAD, THEIR THINKING BECAME NONSENSE, AND THEIR SENSELESS MINDS WERE DARKENED. CLAIMING TO BE WISE, THEY BECAME FOOLS AND EXCHANGED THE GLORY OF THE IMMORTAL GOD FOR IMAGES RESEMBLING MORTAL MAN, BIRDS, FOUR-FOOTED ANIMALS, AND REPTILES. *ROMANS 1:21-23*

When was the last time you longed to be embraced by a bird, a wild animal, or a reptile when you were hurting? The concept is foolish. Those who turn from God to embrace a God-substitute suffer terrible loss. Why? Because they were made to find joy in God, not the substitute. They swap God's present and future blessing for something they can immediately see, taste, or feel. But that something never satisfies.

**Name some of the things people substitute
for a relationship with God.**

_____   _____   _____

_____   _____   _____

I've done it. So have you. Money, success, ego, pleasure, power, sex—the list of God-substitutes is endless. To one degree or another, all sinners trade what they have—and could have had— for a lie. Sometimes the lies get bigger and the stakes get higher as our lives inch toward destruction. In the case of sexual immorality, we willingly trade our future blessings to fulfill some hormonal urge or some secret fantasy.

**Read Romans 1:26-31 in your Bible. List some of the things
for which people were exchanging God's truth.**

_____

_____

It's always a terrible trade, a deal with the Devil, who never keeps his bargains. Each day men and women forfeit future happiness for the sake of temporary sexual stimulation. Like drug addicts, we go from fix to fix, trading the contentment of righteous living for the quick hits that always leave us empty, craving more.

Notice that Paul was describing people who should have known better. Through the years God had revealed His character, His ways, and His laws to the world so that people would know who He is.

**In each of the following verses, underline evidence
that the people had a knowledge of God.**

THOUGH THEY KNEW GOD, THEY DID NOT GLORIFY HIM AS GOD OR SHOW GRATITUDE. *ROMANS 1:21*

BECAUSE THEY DID NOT THINK IT WORTHWHILE TO HAVE GOD IN THEIR KNOWLEDGE, GOD DELIVERED THEM OVER TO A WORTHLESS MIND TO DO WHAT IS MORALLY WRONG. *ROMANS 1:28*

ALTHOUGH THEY KNOW FULL WELL GOD'S JUST SENTENCE—THAT THOSE WHO PRACTICE SUCH THINGS DESERVE TO DIE—THEY NOT ONLY DO THEM, BUT EVEN APPLAUD OTHERS WHO PRACTICE THEM. *ROMANS 1:32*

Because the people Paul described knew God, they knew that their actions were wrong. They even knew that they deserved death for their sins! Yet they chose idols over God and even supported others who acted the same way.

Like the people in Romans 1, believers today know that when we choose immorality, we are holding on to an idol, a God-substitute. Can you see the absurdity of choosing a material object, a wrong behavior, or a harmful relationship over the blessing of honoring God?

Write the Purity Principle, which you learned in day 1.

_____

Speaking of smart choices, let's revisit Jonah in the belly of the fish. Read Jonah 2:9 to discover how Jonah chose not to hang on to idols:

I WILL SACRIFICE TO YOU
WITH A VOICE OF THANKSGIVING.
I WILL FULFILL WHAT I HAVE VOWED.
SALVATION IS FROM THE LORD! JONAH 2:9

Jonah resolved to fulfill what he had vowed to God: to preach the gospel to the people of Nineveh. After running from God, he chose to obey. Nothing like a few days of being fish food for Jonah to realize that God's way is always best.

Have you substituted an idol for a walk of purity with God?
❏ Yes   ❏ No
If so, what are you trading for this idol?

_____

State what is needed for you to become obedient.

_____

THE DAY IN REVIEW

**Review today's lesson.
What was the most important concept you read today?**

_____

_____

How will this truth challenge you to be like Christ?

_____

_____

**Think about any idols you have substituted for a walk of purity with God. If you are ready, confess and destroy them. If not, pray each day that God will help you fulfill your vow to follow Christ as Lord in all areas of your life.
Write your prayer below.**

_____

_____

_____

_____

_____

_____

The Truth About Consequences

day 4

Eric stormed into my office and flopped into a chair. "I'm really mad at God." Having grown up in a strong church family, he had married a Christian girl and had a daughter. Young and gifted, Eric once brimmed with potential. Now he was the picture of misery.

"OK, so why are you mad at God?"

"Because," he said, "last week I committed adultery."

After a long pause I finally said: "I can see why God would be mad at you. But why are you mad at God?"

Eric explained that for several months he and a woman in his office had felt a strong, mutual attraction to each other. He had earnestly prayed that God would keep him from immorality.

"Did you ask your wife to pray for you?" I asked. "Did you stay away from the woman?"

"Well, no. We went out for lunch almost every day."

Slowly I started pushing a book across my desk. Eric watched, uncomprehending, as the book inched closer to the edge. I prayed aloud, "Lord, please keep this book from falling!"

I kept pushing and praying. God didn't suspend the law of gravity. The book went right over the edge, smacking the floor.

"I'm mad at God," I said to Eric. "I asked Him to keep my book from falling, but He let me down!"

I can still hear the sound of that book hitting the floor. It was the sound of Eric's life when it came crashing down.

Eric's story didn't end that day. Eventually he became a sexual predator, molesting his own daughter. He's been in prison for years now, repentant but suffering the consequences of inching his life toward the edge until gravity took over.

Not everyone who commits adultery becomes a sexual predator and ends up in prison, but how many Christians hope that God will guard us from calamity and misery, while every day we make small, seemingly inconsequential immoral choices that inch us toward bigger immoralities?

Check examples of seemingly inconsequential immoral choices that can lead to disaster.
- ❏ Viewing a pornographic Web site
- ❏ Viewing a sexually explicit movie or video
- ❏ Fantasizing about someone in your workplace
- ❏ Setting boundaries for intimacy on dates
- ❏ Looking at pictures that feed sexual thoughts

With every little choice that fuels our lust, we push ourselves closer to the edge. Our holy God made the universe in such a way that actions true to His character and to His laws are always rewarded. Actions that violate His character are always punished. God rewards every act of justice; He punishes every act of injustice.

That doesn't mean God always intervenes directly. The punishment is built into the sin. Shame, degradation, and warping of the personality naturally follow. We get to choose our own path. But each path leads to inevitable consequences.

Write the Purity Principle again.

Purity is safe. Impurity is risky. Purity always helps us. Impurity always hurts us. Count on it. Consider Jesus' story about two men who made different choices:

EVERYONE WHO HEARS THESE WORDS OF MINE AND ACTS ON THEM WILL BE LIKE A SENSIBLE MAN WHO BUILT HIS HOUSE ON THE ROCK. THE RAIN FELL, THE RIVERS ROSE, AND THE WINDS BLEW AND POUNDED THAT HOUSE. YET IT DIDN'T COLLAPSE, BECAUSE ITS FOUNDATION WAS ON THE ROCK. BUT EVERYONE WHO HEARS THESE WORDS OF MINE AND DOESN'T ACT ON THEM WILL BE LIKE A FOOLISH MAN WHO BUILT HIS HOUSE ON THE SAND. THE RAIN FELL, THE RIVERS ROSE, THE WINDS BLEW AND POUNDED THAT HOUSE, AND IT COLLAPSED. AND ITS COLLAPSE WAS GREAT! *MATTHEW 7:24-27*

Underline the two outcomes for these men.

The first man's house didn't collapse, because it was built on the rock! You don't have to be an architect or an engineer to understand how sensible—smart—it is to build a structure on a firm foundation. Conversely, it is foolish—stupid—to build anything on sand and expect it to stand.

Jesus measures obedience not by its virtue but by its wisdom. He measures disobedience not by its wrongness but by its foolishness. The foolish man doomed himself to a great collapse by his own stupid decision. The obedient man isn't called righteous but sensible. He was just being smart.

Satan's greatest victories and our biggest defeats come when he gets us to ask, "Should I choose what God commands me, or should I do what's best for me?" We will not consistently choose God's way until we understand that His way is always best for us.

The Book of Proverbs teaches the wisdom of sexual purity, while emphasizing the consequences of sexual impurity:

WHY, MY SON, WOULD YOU BE INFATUATED
WITH A FORBIDDEN WOMAN
OR WHY EMBRACE THE BREAST OF A STRANGER?
FOR A MAN'S WAYS ARE BEFORE THE LORD'S EYES,
AND HE CONSIDERS ALL HIS PATHS.
A WICKED MAN'S INIQUITIES ENTRAP HIM;
HE IS ENTANGLED IN THE ROPES OF HIS OWN SIN.
HE WILL DIE BECAUSE THERE IS NO INSTRUCTION,
AND BE LOST BECAUSE OF HIS GREAT STUPIDITY. *PROVERBS 5:20-23*

**In these verses underline the consequences
of saying yes to impurity.**

"Entangled in the ropes of his own sin," this man is the primary victim of his foolishness. Just look at Eric. He will have to live with the consequences of his choice for the rest of his life.

List some consequences of Eric's immoral choices.

_____

Eric forfeited a wife who loved him; a daughter who would have adored him; and the respect of his family, friends, co-workers, and church. In the end Eric forfeited his freedom.

A believer recovering from sexual addiction told me: "Addicts always think they can get away with it. You won't change until you realize you can't." I can never get away with sexual immorality. There will always be consequences. God wants me to remember that—for my sake.

THE DAY IN REVIEW

Review today's lesson.
What was the most important concept you read today?

_____

How will this truth challenge you to be like Christ?

_____

**Think about the consequences of impure actions
you are tempted to take. God has graciously established
moral consequences as warnings about our behavior.
Thank Him for this provision. Ask for His strength and
wisdom to remain sexually pure. Write your prayer below.**

_____
_____
_____
_____

The Choice Is Yours

One night as a young pastor I chose to view pornography. Afterward I felt terrible, having failed my Lord, my wife, and my church. I had been a fool. I caught a horrifying glimpse of what I could easily become. But shame did nothing to deliver me. I had to start thinking—and choosing—differently.

Look at the ultimate consequence of impure choices:

HE [THE SEXUALLY IMPURE] FOLLOWS HER IMPULSIVELY
LIKE AN OX GOING TO THE SLAUGHTER,
LIKE A DEER BOUNDING TOWARD A TRAP
UNTIL AN ARROW PIERCES ITS LIVER,
LIKE A BIRD DARTING INTO A SNARE—
HE DOESN'T KNOW IT WILL COST HIM HIS LIFE. *PROVERBS 7:22-23*

What is the result described? _____

Someone who pursues impurity doesn't know it will cost him his life. When we address our choices in the area of sexual purity, we are talking about life-or-death decisions.

Do you really want to be like an ox going to slaughter, a deer running toward a trap, or a bird heading for a snare? If so, keep flirting with the man next door or the new receptionist at the office. Keep thinking impure thoughts about the girl or boy who sits beside you in class. Keep watching those television commercials and sitcoms and movies that shoot sex at you like arrows. You're headed for the slaughterhouse:

HE [THE WICKED MAN] WILL DIE FOR LACK OF DISCIPLINE,
LED ASTRAY BY HIS OWN GREAT FOLLY. *PROVERBS 5:23, NIV*

The folly of impurity doesn't just lead to unhappiness or disappointment. It leads to death!

It's OK to be out there for yourself on this issue. It's right to guard your virginity. It's fitting to hold out the prospect of grief and self-destruction as reasons to avoid impurity.

A church leader admitted: "There have been times when I've had serious temptations toward adultery. I'd like to say that my love for God and for my wife were enough to keep me from falling. But it came down to sheer terror. I was certain that if I traveled that road, God would let my life turn miserable."

He's a wise man who acted in his own best interest. He knows that impurity leads to self-destruction and that purity will be rewarded with heaven's payoffs. Recognizing what was at stake, this brother never disobeyed God or shamed his church. He never trashed his ministry. He never broke his wife's heart or devastated his children.

Mark each statement *T* for *true* or *F* for *false*.

___ Those who choose purity are acting in their best interest.

___ Those who choose impurity think it is in their best interest.

___ Those who choose impurity never act in their best interest.

All of those are true. Remember Lucinda, Tiffany, Kyle, and Eric? Those who have succumbed to sexual temptation did not do so in their self-interest. Rather, they pursued what Satan deceived them into thinking was their self-interest. Had they pursued their true self-interest, they would have run from temptation and embraced purity as a drowning person grabs a life preserver. And how different their lives and families would have been.

When God calls you to pursue purity, He is not asking you to do what will deprive you of joy but what will bring you the greatest joy. To choose purity is to put yourself under God's blessing. To choose impurity is to put yourself under God's curse.

Addressing God's delivered people, Moses succinctly described every person's choice to live in obedience or disobedience to God:

I CALL HEAVEN AND EARTH AS WITNESSES AGAINST YOU TODAY THAT I HAVE SET BEFORE YOU LIFE AND DEATH, BLESSING AND CURSE. CHOOSE LIFE SO THAT YOU AND YOUR DESCENDANTS MAY LIVE, LOVE THE LORD YOUR GOD, OBEY HIM, AND REMAIN FAITHFUL TO HIM. FOR HE IS YOUR LIFE.
DEUTERONOMY 30:19-20

We can choose life or death. We can choose blessings—joy, peace, life, hope, and laughter. Or we can choose curses—misery, scars, and a handful of ashes.

It's your decision. You cast your vote with every choice.

What's your voting record?
Check the prayer that your choices are uttering.
❏ "God, bless me for obeying You."
❏ "God, curse me for disobeying You."

THE DAY IN REVIEW

Review today's lesson.
What was the most important concept you read today?

_____

How will this truth challenge you to be like Christ?

_____

Pray and commit to God that you will choose His blessings by walking in purity from this point forward.
Write your prayer below.

_____
_____
_____
_____
_____

week 2

day 1

What's the Big Deal About Sex?

The Power of Sex

Have you heard the saying "All sin is alike to God"? Not according to the Apostle Paul. He said to people in sex-saturated Corinth:

FLEE FROM SEXUAL IMMORALITY! "EVERY SIN A PERSON COMMITS IS OUTSIDE THE BODY," BUT THE PERSON WHO IS SEXUALLY IMMORAL SINS AGAINST HIS OWN BODY. *1 CORINTHIANS 6:18*

What do you think Paul meant by the distinction he made?

_____

_____

Something is qualitatively different about sexual sin because sex is not just something you do; sex is someone you are. When you have sex, you put your life on the line. You give away something you will never get back. Purity and impurity are more than external issues of behavior, culture, and practice. They cut to the living core of who you are and who you will become.

Sex wasn't invented by Hollywood, Madonna, or a pervert in an Internet chat room. Sex was created by an infinitely holy God. The Book of Genesis tells us that God created the first man and the first woman in His image and gave them responsibilities:

BE FRUITFUL, MULTIPLY, FILL THE EARTH, AND SUBDUE IT. RULE THE FISH OF THE SEA, THE BIRDS OF THE SKY, AND EVERY CREATURE THAT CRAWLS ON THE EARTH. *GENESIS 1:28*

Underline the duties in this verse that relate to sexual union.

Genesis 1:31 says that God saw all He had made and deemed it "very good." Sex was part of the all that was very good. God designed sex as part of His good creation, intending it as the way a married man and woman would be fruitful, multiply, and fill the earth.

God also intended sex to bring pleasure to a married couple. Read what Solomon wrote about his beloved:

HOW BEAUTIFUL YOU ARE AND HOW PLEASING,
O LOVE, WITH YOUR DELIGHTS!
YOUR STATURE IS LIKE THAT OF THE PALM,
AND YOUR BREASTS LIKE CLUSTERS OF FRUIT.
I SAID, "I WILL CLIMB THE PALM TREE;
I WILL TAKE HOLD OF ITS FRUIT."
MAY YOUR BREASTS BE LIKE THE CLUSTERS OF THE VINE,
THE FRAGRANCE OF YOUR BREATH LIKE APPLES,
AND YOUR MOUTH LIKE THE BEST WINE. *SONG OF SONGS 7:6-9, NIV*

Solomon's vivid word pictures express the powerful emotions associated with sexual desire. Sex is incredibly powerful; it can do immense good or immense harm. Although God designed sex for our good, people can choose to use it in ways that bring harm and destruction. In this respect, sex is a lot like fire.

Indicate the beneficial and harmful ways fire can be used by writing *B* or *H* in each blank.

___ Campfire ___ Fireplace ___ Forest fire
___ Arson ___ For cooking ___ To give light

God's most magnificent gifts, taken outside their God-intended boundaries, become utterly ruinous. As long as fire is contained in the fireplace, it keeps you warm. But if fire is set free, the house burns down. So it is with sex. Its potential for great good has a flipside—potential for great evil.

Check some of the devastating and painful effects of sex outside the boundaries of marriage.

❏ Good reputation ❏ Sexually transmitted disease
❏ Unplanned pregnancy ❏ Joy of living in God's will
❏ Loss of virginity ❏ Loss of intimacy in marriage
❏ Emotional hurt ❏ Severed relationship with God

I've walked through the smoldering ruins of lives that have been devastated by immorality. I have shared their despair as they wondered whether they can ever rebuild. (They can, but believing they can is another matter.) The scenes are permanently imprinted in my mind. The power of sex to destroy makes the Purity Principle vitally important.

Write the Purity Principle below.

_____

In contrast to the destructive potential of sex outside God's boundaries, to embrace God's ideal for sexual purity is to claim a magnificent gift that God provided for our benefit and enjoyment. Purity is beautiful, like the fragrance of a rose after a summer shower. And its beauty will never end for those who are in Christ. All who live in heaven will be pure:

NOTHING IMPURE WILL EVER ENTER IT [THE NEW JERUSALEM], NOR WILL ANYONE WHO DOES WHAT IS SHAMEFUL OR DECEITFUL, BUT ONLY THOSE WHOSE NAMES ARE WRITTEN IN THE LAMB'S BOOK OF LIFE. *REVELATION 21:27, NIV*

Check the statement that most closely reflects your view.
❏ I accept God's plan to limit sex to a married man and woman.
❏ I think God's plan for sex is too restrictive.

THE DAY IN REVIEW

Review today's lesson.
What was the most important concept you read today?

_____

_____

How will this truth challenge you to be like Christ?

_____

_____

**Admit to God any attitudes or actions in your life
that represent a harmful view of sex.
Ask for His forgiveness. Commit to accept and live
by God's ideal for sex. Write your prayer below.**

_____

_____

_____

_____

_____

God's Boundaries for Sex

day 2

According to the Bible, the boundaries of sex are the boundaries of marriage. Sexual union is intended as an expression of a life-long commitment. Apart from marriage the lasting commitment is absent, so the sex act becomes a lie.

To claim the privilege apart from the responsibility perverts God's intention. Every act of sex outside marriage cheapens both sex and marriage. Sex is a privilege inseparable from the responsibilities of the sacred marriage covenant.

God designed sex to be the joining of a man and a woman—the joining of two spirits, not just two bodies. Sex should be given to someone to whom you are 100 percent committed (as measured by legal marriage), not taken from someone to whom you are uncommitted.

"But we really love each other" is one reason people give for having sex outside marriage. What are other reasons?

_____

_____

These reasons have no bearing on the godly ethics of sexual intimacy. Sex does not become permissible through subjective feelings but only through the objective, lifelong commitment of marriage. Those are God's rules, and we can do nothing to change them. When we break them, they always break us.

God's moral laws are like guardrails on a road. They are there not to punish or deprive us but to protect us, standing between us and destruction. Therefore, a smart traveler doesn't curse guardrails. He doesn't whine, "That guardrail dented my fender!" He looks over the cliff, sees demolished vehicles, and thanks God for guardrails that protected him.

Pause and thank God for straightforwardly presenting His boundaries about sexual purity in His Word.

Staying within the boundaries means staying in God's will. How many times have you heard people talk about finding God's will? We speak of God's will as if it were lost or as though it were a Rubik's Cube that takes many years and the brains of Einstein to unravel. But you don't have to wonder where God stands on sex outside marriage. For example, Paul wrote a highly charged paragraph on sexual purity that resounds with the smart-versus-stupid theme:

IT IS GOD'S WILL THAT YOU SHOULD BE SANCTIFIED: THAT YOU SHOULD AVOID SEXUAL IMMORALITY; THAT EACH OF YOU SHOULD LEARN TO CONTROL HIS OWN BODY IN A WAY THAT IS HOLY AND HONORABLE, NOT IN PASSIONATE LUST LIKE THE HEATHEN, WHO DO NOT KNOW GOD. ... THE LORD WILL PUNISH MEN FOR ALL SUCH SINS, AS WE HAVE ALREADY TOLD YOU AND WARNED YOU. FOR GOD DID NOT CALL US TO BE IMPURE, BUT TO LIVE A HOLY LIFE. THEREFORE, HE WHO REJECTS THIS INSTRUCTION DOES NOT REJECT MAN BUT GOD, WHO GIVES YOU HIS HOLY SPIRIT. *1 THESSALONIANS 4:3-8, NIV*

This passage is clear on God's will for sexual purity.

According to this passage, what is God's will about sexual immorality?
- ❏ It's OK just this once.
- ❏ Avoid it.
- ❏ It's OK as long as you don't get caught.

You don't have to search for anything obscure or hidden in Paul's instruction. The word *avoid* is quite clear!

People search for God's will, but many of those same people don't bother to live by what Scripture says is His will. It is fruitless to seek God's will in other ways while ignoring what He has already told us in His Word.

Paul used an important phrase in this passage:

... LEARN TO CONTROL HIS OWN BODY. *1 THESSALONIANS 4:4, NIV*

Circle the first word of this phrase.

The process of controlling your body doesn't come naturally; otherwise, you wouldn't have to learn it. It requires training and discipline. Paul used the same idea in writing to the people in the church at Corinth:

EVERYONE WHO COMPETES EXERCISES SELF-CONTROL IN EVERYTHING. HOWEVER, THEY DO IT TO RECEIVE A PERISHABLE CROWN, BUT WE AN IMPER-ISHABLE ONE. THEREFORE I DO NOT RUN LIKE ONE WHO RUNS AIMLESSLY, OR BOX LIKE ONE WHO BEATS THE AIR. INSTEAD, I DISCIPLINE MY BODY AND BRING IT UNDER STRICT CONTROL, SO THAT AFTER PREACHING TO OTHERS, I MYSELF WILL NOT BE DISQUALIFIED. *1 CORINTHIANS 9:25-27*

Paul used the analogies of running and boxing to demonstrate the concept of discipline in the Christian life. Just as someone competing in either sport doesn't go into an event without the discipline of training, neither can a Christian control his own body without training and discipline.

I have a friend who runs. He recently ran a marathon. Did he decide one day to take on a marathon? No! It was the discipline of running consistently—regardless of weather or other conditions—that got him there. Does this friend like to get up at 4:30 every morning to run before work? Not really. It's a matter of will. The marathon number displayed in his office remind hims of the race he ran and the discipline it took to get him there.

How can someone learn discipline for a life of sexual purity?

❏ Read God's Word.
❏ Pray.
❏ Hang out with people who have sex outside marriage.
❏ Watch sexually stimulating movies.
❏ Set boundaries for your sexual behavior.
❏ Listen to sexually explicit music.
❏ Read books on sexual purity.

Let's examine another phrase Paul used in 1 Thessalonians:

... NOT IN PASSIONATE LUST LIKE THE HEATHEN. *1 THESSALONIANS 4:5, NIV*

Christ's disciples did not live by lust, which truly set them apart—or sanctified them—from the pagan culture around them. Apparently, many people in Thessalonica didn't live by God's standards and boundaries, especially those for sexual purity.

The problem Paul identified here wasn't passion but lust. How can a person be passionate and not be lustful? Let's compare these words.

Look up the definition of *passion* and write it here.

_____

Look up the definition of *lust* and write it here.

_____

Compare the two. What is the main difference?

_____

Passion merely refers to a strong emotion, while *lust* designates unbridled sexual desire or craving. In the Bible, lust is never mentioned in a positive way. Sometimes biblical writers placed the word *passionate* before it for emphasis.

Name three things you are passionate about.

_____   _____

_____

Did you include God?   ❏ Yes   ❏ No

We need to cultivate our passions for the right object, not the wrong ones. We serve a passionate God. We should love and serve Him passionately.

Do you want to do God's will? Then embrace purity. Recognize God's boundaries for sex. Learn to control your body. Refuse to take sexual advantage of anyone. In so doing, you will avoid God's punishment and taste the joy of a life that pleases Him.

THE DAY IN REVIEW

Review today's lesson.
What was the most important concept you read today?

_____

_____

How will this truth challenge you to be like Christ?

_____

_____

Ask God to help you learn self-control and to give you a passion for Him and His will. Commit to honor the boundaries He has established to keep you walking in His will. Write your prayer below.

_____

_____

_____

_____

_____

_____

Under Attack

Sometimes when I'm speaking on purity, I borrow a pencil from an audience member, break it, and stomp on it. The audience reacts with shock, thinking I broke someone else's pencil. Then I explain that it really was my pencil, which I gave to the person in advance. That changes everything. Because it belongs to me, I have the right to do with it as I please. If it belonged to someone else, I would not have this right.

This concept applies to the way we view our bodies. To whom does my body belong? Paul said it belongs to God:

DO YOU NOT KNOW THAT YOUR BODY IS A SANCTUARY OF THE HOLY SPIRIT WHO IS IN YOU, WHOM YOU HAVE FROM GOD? YOU ARE NOT YOUR OWN, FOR YOU WERE BOUGHT AT A PRICE; THEREFORE GLORIFY GOD IN YOUR BODY.
1 CORINTHIANS 6:19-20

When I came to Christ, the title of my life transferred to God. I was bought and paid for. I belong to Him.

Because God owns your body, how should you treat it?
❏ Take good care of it.
❏ Honor His demand for sexual purity.
❏ Do what you want without thinking about the cost.
❏ Use your body to satisfy your desires.
❏ Use your body for God's glory.

God's shed blood purchased me. I am His by creation and by redemption. He has every right to tell me what to do with my mind and body. I have no right to do whatever I want with them. Because God always acts not only for His glory but also for my best interest, I can fully trust that whatever He forbids will hurt me and whatever He commands will benefit me.

35

If you are a Christian, you belong to Christ. That makes you a targeted man or woman. The forces of evil have taken out a contract on you. Satan is out to get you. If he can't take you to hell, he will do his best to make your life a hell on earth.

I learned a long time ago that if Satan is out to get me, I'd better take it seriously. I remember with embarrassment that when I was a Bible-college student, I heard of a prominent Christian leader who had committed adultery. I thought I could never betray the Lord and my wife that way. Not me.

By God's grace I've never had sex with anyone but my wife. But this is largely due to the fact that I wised up. I came to grips with a frightening truth: it really could happen to me. And I'd been a fool to think otherwise.

If you assume you'll never be burglarized, you'll leave the windows open and cash lying out. If you think you'll never fall morally, you'll live carelessly, failing to take precautions.

Check examples of precautions you could take to remain morally pure.

❑ Avoid places where temptation is strongest.
❑ Avoid persons to whom you are inappropriately attracted.
❑ Ask God to protect you even though you fantasize about someone else's spouse.
❑ Go ahead and flirt; you know where to draw the line.
❑ Get rid of sexual videos and magazines.
❑ Stay out of compromising situations.
❑ Other: _____

I know of Christian leaders who travel extensively. To prevent temptation, they keep men around them to whom they are accountable at all times.

Some Christian companies have set guardrails to help their employees avoid moral traps. They don't allow employees of the opposite gender to travel together, to be in the same lodging, or to rent just one automobile for their local travel.

What guardrail can you put up in your workplace to help keep you pure?

Don't kid yourself that it can never happen to you; it can. And if you don't think it can, it almost certainly will.

As a pastor I was counseling a woman when it suddenly struck me that she was interested in me. And here's what frightened me: I had sensed this from the beginning, but I had been flattered by her attention.

Because I wasn't (yet) emotionally involved with her, I was tempted to rationalize: at this stage it was harmless. Deep down, though, I heard an alarm. I knew I was walking in a field laced with land mines. God reminded me that every adultery I knew of had begun with something that seemed harmless.

So I ran. I made other arrangements. She could continue counseling with someone else. My decision may have offended her, but it was a small price.

Where or when does Satan attack you most?

We tend to be most vulnerable when we're tired, isolated, lonely, discouraged, depressed, angry, or struggling in our relationships, especially with our mates. Don't think for a moment that demons don't know this or will hesitate to pounce on us in those very times. Satan did it to Jesus. Although Jesus was prepared, Satan didn't accept Jesus' victory as total defeat:

WHEN THE DEVIL HAD FINISHED ALL THIS TEMPTING, HE LEFT HIM UNTIL AN OPPORTUNE TIME. *LUKE 4:13, NIV*

Paul's warning deserves a prominent place on our dashboards, desks, calendars, and personal digital assistants:

37

WHOEVER THINKS HE STANDS MUST BE CAREFUL NOT TO FALL!
1 CORINTHIANS 10:12

**Write Paul's warning on a three-by-five-inch card.
Post it in a place where you can be reminded of its wisdom.**

Always remember whose you are. But also remember that Satan's assault on your purity will be relentless. If you think you don't need to take precautions, you can spell your name S-t-u-p-i-d.

Name a precaution you need to take to avoid sexual sin.

_____

THE DAY IN REVIEW

**Review today's lesson.
What was the most important concept you read today?**

_____

How will this truth challenge you to be like Christ?

_____

**Ask God to help you live as His possession,
bought with the blood of His Son, and to help you
glorify Him through your body. Ask Him to alert you
and protect you when times of temptation come
so that you can run to Him. Write your prayer below.**

_____

_____

_____

_____

_____

_____

Reaping What You Sow

God designed His universe in such a way that moral or immoral behavior is eventually exposed for what it is. Violating God's moral standards is like violating the law of gravity. You can't get away with it. You reap what you sow:

day 4

DON'T BE UNDER ANY ILLUSION: YOU CANNOT MAKE A FOOL OF GOD! A MAN'S HARVEST IN LIFE WILL DEPEND ENTIRELY ON WHAT HE SOWS. IF HE SOWS FOR HIS OWN LOWER NATURE HIS HARVEST WILL BE THE DECAY AND DEATH OF HIS OWN NATURE. BUT IF HE SOWS FOR THE SPIRIT HE WILL REAP THE HARVEST OF EVERLASTING LIFE BY THAT SPIRIT. *GALATIANS 6:7-8, PHILLIPS*

What are the consequences of sowing for your lower nature?
❑ Decay and death   ❑ Life and health

God's Word warns that sooner or later, sexual sin will be exposed:

BE SURE YOUR SIN WILL CATCH UP WITH YOU. *NUMBERS 32:23*
THE ONE WHO LIVES WITH INTEGRITY LIVES SECURELY,
BUT WHOEVER PERVERTS HIS WAYS WILL BE FOUND OUT. *PROVERBS 10:9*
THERE IS NOTHING COVERED THAT WON'T BE UNCOVERED, NOTHING HIDDEN THAT WON'T BE MADE KNOWN. THEREFORE WHATEVER YOU HAVE SAID IN THE DARK WILL BE HEARD IN THE LIGHT, AND WHAT YOU HAVE WHISPERED IN AN EAR IN PRIVATE ROOMS WILL BE PROCLAIMED ON THE HOUSETOPS. *LUKE 12:2-3*

Jesus warned that there's no such thing as a private moment. Imagine having what you've said in private plastered on billboards, printed in the daily newspapers, and broadcast on the evening news.

Have you done anything in private that you would not want proclaimed in public? ❑ Yes ❑ No

One of Satan's oldest tactics is to weave a phony web of secrecy, casting an illusion of privacy over our sinful choices. He tells us: "No one is watching. No one will know." But he's lying. Someone is watching—the Audience of One. Someone already knows. And in time others will know.

Name some ways society has devised to hide some of the consequences of sexual impurity.

_____

_____

We never get away with anything. Antibiotics prevent or cure some sexually transmitted diseases. Contraceptives reduce the chances of pregnancy. But there is no contraceptive for the conscience. Medical science may eliminate some consequences of my sin, but it cannot remove my accountability to God:

ANYONE WHO TURNS HIS EAR FROM HEARING THE LAW—
EVEN HIS PRAYER IS DETESTABLE. *PROVERBS 28:9*

If we are not practicing purity, we nullify our prayers and our ministry. Sexual sin blocks fellowship with God. If we are in immorality's grip, there's only one prayer God wants to hear—a prayer of confession and repentance.

Look at the example of King David in the Bible. Instead of going to war, David stayed home. He watched a neighbor's beautiful wife bathe on her rooftop, sent for her, and had sex with her. After she told him she was pregnant, David had her husband put on the front lines and killed (see 2 Sam. 11).

God sent the prophet Nathan to talk to David. Nathan confronted the king by telling him a story.

**Read Nathan's story in 2 Samuel 12:1-4 in your Bible.
Then record from verses 5-6 David's reaction.**

_____

Nathan responded with God's words in verse 7: " 'You are the
man!' " Then Nathan delivered a blistering description of David's
sin (see vv. 8-10), followed by God's curse on David's family:

I AM GOING TO BRING DISASTER ON YOU FROM YOUR OWN FAMILY: I WILL
TAKE YOUR WIVES AND GIVE THEM TO ANOTHER BEFORE YOUR VERY EYES,
AND HE WILL SLEEP WITH THEM PUBLICLY. YOU ACTED IN SECRET, BUT I WILL
DO THIS BEFORE ALL ISRAEL AND IN BROAD DAYLIGHT. ... BECAUSE YOU
TREATED THE LORD WITH SUCH CONTEMPT IN THIS MATTER, THE SON BORN
TO YOU WILL DIE. *2 SAMUEL 12:11-12,14*

**Underline the severe consequences of David's sin.
Circle the word that describes how David thought
he could get away with his actions.**

Notice that David didn't think he could get away with his actions
because he was the king but because he had acted in secret.
David knew that he had sinned. Read verse 13:

DAVID RESPONDED TO NATHAN, "I HAVE SINNED AGAINST THE LORD."
2 SAMUEL 12:13

Against whom had David sinned? _____

God is sovereign in each person's life, but an individual's private
sins can bring terrible consequences on others. Let's read a
modern-day story about a child whose father's sexual sins
seriously affected her.

41

Cindy was 12 when her father, a church leader, committed adultery with a woman in the church and left his family. Deeply hurt, Cindy's godly mother hastily and unwisely remarried an unbeliever. Cindy had to live with looks of pity and scorn wherever she went. But it gets worse. Cindy has experienced a long series of destructive relationships with men, including repeated sexual compromises. Though fully responsible for her own actions, she is also reaping what her father sowed. Unfortunately, Cindy's children, grandchildren, and great-grandchildren could be affected by her father's sin:

I, THE LORD YOUR GOD, AM A JEALOUS GOD, PUNISHING THE CHILDREN FOR THE FATHERS' SIN, TO THE THIRD AND FOURTH [GENERATIONS] OF THOSE WHO HATE ME. *EXODUS 20:5*

We inevitably reap what we sow. God gave His laws to guide us into His will, which is always best for us. When we go against His will and disobey Him, we reap what we sow in the form of very serious consequences.

Check some consequences reaped from sexual impurity.
- ❑ Disease
- ❑ Closer family relationships
- ❑ Broken relationships
- ❑ God's blessing
- ❑ Broken fellowship with God
- ❑ The respect of other believers
- ❑ The loss of rewards in heaven
- ❑ The misery of being outside God's will
- ❑ Other: _____

Conversely, when we obey God and do His will, we reap an abundant life filled with all the blessings God has promised. For this reason Paul admonished the people in Galatia,

LET US NOT GROW TIRED OF DOING GOOD, FOR, UNLESS WE THROW IN OUR HAND, THE ULTIMATE HARVEST IS ASSURED. *GALATIANS 6:9, PHILLIPS*

What do you think Paul meant by *the ultimate harvest?*

_____

Our goal is that ultimate harvest—a life that pleases God and the reward of His blessings for all eternity. Don't give up doing good, my friend. It's so worth it!

Check one: I am reaping a harvest of—
❏ decay and death; ❏ God's blessings.

THE DAY IN REVIEW

Review today's lesson.
What was the most important concept you read today?

_____

How will this truth challenge you to be like Christ?

_____

Ask God to help you reap the harvest of a good and pure life that pleases Him. Confess anything you have done in private that you would not want proclaimed in public. Ask God to remind you when you are tempted that there are no private moments. Write your prayer below.

_____
_____
_____
_____
_____
_____

The Voice of Temptation

day 5

Even though we are saved, our fleshly human nature continually influences us to sin. Satan wants us to deny our spiritual nature and to act from our sinful nature. Sexual immorality is one expression of sin with which he tempts us:

THE WORKS OF THE FLESH ARE OBVIOUS: SEXUAL IMMORALITY, MORAL IMPURITY, PROMISCUITY. *GALATIANS 5:19*

Scripture is clear that Satan is on the attack:

BE SOBER! BE ON THE ALERT! YOUR ADVERSARY THE DEVIL IS PROWLING AROUND LIKE A ROARING LION, LOOKING FOR ANYONE HE CAN DEVOUR. *1 PETER 5:8*

When a sexually provocative image appears, I envision a barbed fishhook at the end of a line. If I hesitate—even think about nibbling—I'll be caught and reeled in. The lure, of course, is beautiful. How else would our enemy hook us? Temptations always look good; otherwise, they wouldn't be temptations.

Jesus called Satan " 'a liar and the father of liars' " (John 8:44). God warned the first humans that if they ate the forbidden fruit, they would die. How did Satan counter God's words?

"NO! YOU WILL NOT DIE," THE SERPENT SAID TO THE WOMAN. "IN FACT, GOD KNOWS THAT WHEN YOU EAT IT YOUR EYES WILL BE OPENED AND YOU WILL BE LIKE GOD, KNOWING GOOD AND EVIL" *GENESIS 3:4-5*

In essence Satan said that God would be jealous if the humans He created had the same powers as He did. Another big lie.

Instead of having God's powers, what happened after the man and his wife ate the fruit?

Underline the consequences in the verses below.

THE EYES OF BOTH OF THEM WERE OPENED, AND THEY KNEW THEY WERE NAKED; SO THEY SEWED FIG LEAVES TOGETHER AND MADE LOINCLOTHS FOR THEMSELVES. *GENESIS 3:6-7*

Not exactly what Satan had promised.

Every time you are tempted toward sexual sin, you must choose between two voices—God's or Satan's. Which will you believe? When a sexual image lures your mind toward lust, the Devil barrages you with lies: "It will make you feel like a man." "It will relieve your pain, disappointment, and stress." "He really loves you." "It will make you happy." "God is trying to keep something good from you."

What equips you to counter Satan's lies?
❏ Common sense ❏ God's Word ❏ The media

God's Word exposes Satan's lies. The Bible tells you that real happiness can be found only in Christ. If you know Christ, then you also know His voice. Jesus said,

MY SHEEP HEAR MY VOICE, I KNOW THEM, AND THEY FOLLOW ME. *JOHN 10:27*

What are you doing to listen to Jesus' voice?

_____

You must choose between two voices. Trust Satan for temporary pleasure or trust God for abundant life. Choose sexual fantasies or intimacy with God. You cannot have both. The breakthrough comes only when you pursue God, making Him the object of your quest, and when you realize that fantasies are only a cheap God-substitute. Running to them is running from God.

Match Jesus' words with the eternal blessings He offers.

___ 1. "Everyone who believes in Him
will have eternal life" (John 3:15).   a. Peace

___ 2. "God did not send His Son into
the world that He might condemn
the world, but that the world   b. Eternal life
might be saved through Him"
(John 3:17).

___ 3. "You will know the truth, and   c. Heaven
the truth will set you free"
(John 8:32).

___ 4. "Just as I have loved you,   d. Love
you must also love one
another" (John 13:34).

___ 5. "I will come back and   e. Salvation
receive you to Myself,
so that where I am you
may be also" (John 14:4).   f. Truth and
                                                           freedom
___ 6. "I have told you these things
so that in Me you may
have peace" (John 16:33).

___ 7. "I speak these things in   g. Joy
the world so that they may
have My joy completed in
them" (John 17:13).

John Piper wrote: "The fire of lust's pleasures must be fought with the fire of God's pleasures. If we try to fight the fire of lust with prohibitions and threats alone—even the terrible warnings of Jesus—we will fail. We must fight it with a massive promise of superior happiness. We must swallow up the little flicker of lust's pleasure in the conflagration of holy satisfaction."[1]

Choose one of the following. I am pursuing—
❏ lust's pleasures;   ❏ God's pleasures.
Give evidence for your choice from the past week of your life.

_____

THE DAY IN REVIEW

**Review today's lesson.
What was the most important concept you read today?**

_____
_____
_____

How will this truth challenge you to be like Christ?

_____
_____
_____

**Pray about the assessment in the final activity
of today's lesson. Thank God that His Word exposes
Satan's lies. Thank Him for the abundant life He offers
that is superior to temporary sexual pleasure.
Ask Him to help you recognize and listen to
His voice only. Write your prayer below.**

_____
_____
_____
_____
_____
_____

[1]John Piper, *Future Grace* (Sisters, OR: Multnomah Publishers, Inc., 1995), 336.

week 3

The Great Temptation

day 1

The Battle for the Mind

Brad, a seminary student preparing for ministry, argued with his wife one night. Upset, he drove to a coffee shop to think things through. Soon Brad was engrossed in conversation with a young woman. A few hours later he was in bed with her.

Brad came to me, ashamed. "How can I tell my wife? Will she ever forgive me? It was so sudden—there was no warning. It came out of the clear blue sky!"

Or did it? Brad, who had worked nonstop to put himself through seminary, had subtly begun to resent his wife, seeing her and the children as obstacles. He no longer dated her or communicated with her on a deep level. He had been looking at provocative magazines and had been watching raunchy movies. These developments culminated in the horrible episode that seemingly happened without warning.

The truth is, temptation may come suddenly, but sexual sin doesn't. It is the predictable result of natural processes when a relationship is neglected and a mind is exposed to impurity.

Sin doesn't come out of the blue, and neither does moral and spiritual fiber. It results from a process we can control.

Tomorrow's character is made from today's thoughts. We forge our sexual morality through an ongoing series of choices and actions, including tiny indulgences and minuscule compromises. The eye lingers here; the mind loiters there. Like a photographic plate forming an image, our minds accumulate what we expose them to, godly or ungodly. The battle is in our minds.

Like Brad, those who fall to lust's temptation are often taken by surprise. They ask, "Where did that come from?" The Bible gives a clear answer. Read Jesus' words:

FROM THE HEART COME EVIL THOUGHTS, MURDERS, ADULTERIES, SEXUAL IMMORALITIES, THEFTS, FALSE TESTIMONIES, BLASPHEMIES. *MATTHEW 15:19*

Where did Jesus say these things come from? The _____

YOU HAVE HEARD THAT IT WAS SAID, "DO NOT COMMIT ADULTERY." BUT I TELL YOU, EVERYONE WHO LOOKS AT A WOMAN TO LUST FOR HER HAS ALREADY COMMITTED ADULTERY WITH HER IN HIS HEART. *MATTHEW 5:27-28*

Where did Jesus say adultery is committed? In the _____

While the Pharisees emphasized the external, Jesus raised the moral bar by recognizing that lust begins in the heart. It is not only the source of sexual sin but also sin itself. Jesus closed the door to the pharisaical notion that a man could undress a woman in his mind and remain pure.

Lust feeds on whatever we've deposited in our brains—what we've allowed to enter our minds through our senses. The images and words in our minds come either from things our eyes have seen and our ears have heard or from an imaginative conglomerate of this input.

Draw arrows from the words to the brain to identify sources of images and words that deposit information in your brain.

Magazines
Internet
Radio
Flirtatious comments
Jokes

Television
Movies
Conversations
Catalogs
Other: _____

The kind of persons we are becoming is determined by what we take into our brains. We can choose to make certain deposits that incline ourselves toward righteousness.

Draw arrows from the words to the brain to identify sources that deposit information in your brain.

Scripture
Christian books
Christian fellowship

Christ-centered discussion
Ministry to others
Other: _____

The old saying is true: "Sow a thought; reap an action. Sow an action; reap a habit. Sow a habit; reap a character. Sow a character; reap a destiny." Actions, habits, character, and destiny all start with a thought, and thoughts are generated by what we choose to take into our minds. That's why your most important sex organ is your brain.

Lust is centered in the brain; it is mental promiscuity. Getting married doesn't solve the lust problem. A woman who looks at other men still has lust. A man who masturbates still has lust. Men married to beautiful women are just as likely to be addicted to pornography. A lustful person moves from picture to picture, from partner to partner. Lust is a sickness of the soul that gets worse unless repentance and change occur. I include change because many people "repent" again and again and then go back to bondage.

Sexual immorality kills Christian lives and marriages.
We poison ourselves daily, a little at a time: this novel, that
TV show, this movie, that magazine, this calendar, that glance,
this flirtatious comment, that quiet assent to a dirty story.
Because this arsenic of the soul poisons us gradually, we don't
feel much different than yesterday. But we've become very
different than we were five years ago.

**If you struggle with something that is poisoning your mind
and are willing to renounce it, pray: "I know that these sexual
images are poisoning me. Give me the wisdom and resolve
to turn away from them. Turn me to what pleases You."
Write today's date as a reminder of your commitment:**

_____

I have a friend who occasionally drinks nothing but cranberry
juice for one day to flush her physical body of accumulated
toxins. Similarly, in time, by avoiding wrong things and taking
in right things, you can flush harmful influences out of your
system. If you abstain from the poison long enough, something
wonderful happens. Your desire for it decreases. You become
healthy again. This verse will help you implement this concept:

DON'T GET DRUNK WITH WINE, WHICH LEADS TO RECKLESS ACTIONS,
BUT BE FILLED WITH THE SPIRIT. *EPHESIANS 5:18*

**Now reread the verse, replacing the words "don't get drunk
with wine" with "don't dwell on lustful things."**

The principle here is to let God fill your mind with the Holy
Spirit instead of your filling it with anything that would harm
you. Although you can rid your mind of lustful thinking, you
must refill it with something beneficial. If you don't, the same
poison will creep back in and recapture your thoughts.

For decades I've believed that erotic images on television and in movies can poison my mind. I still have a desire to look at them, but that desire is overwhelmed by my resolve to turn away. In fact, turning away has become a deeply ingrained habit. Sometimes I fail but not nearly as often as I did years ago. We are creatures of habit, and God's Spirit can empower us to form new habits.

By choosing to turn away from sexual temptation through God's enabling grace, I choose the path of life and blessing. When I say no to temptation, I say yes to God, and He is pleased and glorified. And no one benefits more than I do.

What will you turn away from in order to say yes to God?

_____

THE DAY IN REVIEW

**Review today's lesson.
What was the most important concept you read today?**

_____

How will this truth challenge you to be like Christ?

_____

_____

**Ask God to help you recognize the powerful effects
of lustful thinking. Ask Him to transform your mind
by helping you remove poisonous thoughts and by
filling you with His Spirit. Write your prayer below.**

_____

_____

_____

_____

_____

_____

Guarding Your Heart

Often we say we want purity, but then we make choices that sabotage it. One man wrote to me: "As someone who self-destructed, I'm quick to warn people of 'gateway' behaviors that often lead to sins with much greater consequences. Occasional masturbation may not seem to warrant radical choices, but where will your sin lead? Will you end up with a friend's wife? With a prostitute? Maybe, if unchecked, 10 years from now you'll be guilty of child sexual abuse, with news trucks pulling onto your front lawn. Sin always escalates."

Choices have consequences. If we want different consequences, we must make different choices. For years I didn't go in a particular doorway to our local supermarket because of a magazine rack. Later, my mental discipline became strong enough that I could keep my eyes diverted. But until then I honored the boundary I had set. It was inconvenient but a small price to pay to guard my purity.

Name a couple of boundaries that could protect sexual purity.

_____   _____

Setting mental boundaries may mean avoiding a checkout line where magazines are displayed, not driving in a certain part of town, or not going on a business trip alone. I can't tell you what your boundaries must be. They vary from person to person.

Boundaries keep temptation from getting a foothold. Our sexual purity cannot grow stronger if we keep doing what we've always done. We must change our habits. We are sentries charged with protecting something immensely strategic. God says,

GUARD YOUR HEART ABOVE ALL ELSE,
FOR IT IS THE SOURCE OF LIFE. *PROVERBS 4:23*

Our hearts are the source of life. If we keep good things in our hearts, good actions will follow. However, if we store up bad things—even things that no one else sees—they will result in bad actions. Read what Jesus had to say about this subject:

A GOOD TREE DOESN'T PRODUCE BAD FRUIT; ON THE OTHER HAND, A BAD TREE DOESN'T PRODUCE GOOD FRUIT. FOR EACH TREE IS KNOWN BY ITS OWN FRUIT. ... A GOOD MAN PRODUCES GOOD OUT OF THE GOOD STOREROOM OF HIS HEART. AN EVIL MAN PRODUCES EVIL OUT OF THE EVIL STOREROOM, FOR HIS MOUTH SPEAKS FROM THE OVERFLOW OF THE HEART. *LUKE 6:43-45*

Our actions result from what we store in our _____.

Because we act from what is stored in our hearts, storing up good things is a high priority—Proverbs 4:23 says "above all else." It is critical that we protect our inmost being from new sources of temptation our enemy could use against us.

Scripture teaches us how to store up good thoughts and reject evil ones:

DO NOT BE CONFORMED TO THIS AGE, BUT BE TRANSFORMED BY THE RENEWING OF YOUR MIND, SO THAT YOU MAY DISCERN WHAT IS THE GOOD, PLEASING, AND PERFECT WILL OF GOD. *ROMANS 12:2*

SET YOUR MINDS ON WHAT IS ABOVE, NOT ON WHAT IS ON THE EARTH. *COLOSSIANS 3:2*

PUT TO DEATH WHATEVER IN YOU IS WORLDLY: SEXUAL IMMORALITY, IMPURITY, LUST, EVIL DESIRE, AND GREED, WHICH IS IDOLATRY. *COLOSSIANS 3:5*

	Reject This	**Do This**
Romans 12:2:	_____	_____
Colossians 3:2:	_____	_____
Colossians 3:5:	_____	_____

Let's do an experiment. Ready? OK. Don't think about snakes. Don't—I repeat, do not—think about big, slimy snakes coming up from your bathtub drain at night and slithering into your bed. You heard me. Don't think about snakes!

Have I kept you from thinking about snakes? No, I've encouraged you to think about them.

Now envision your favorite dessert. Perhaps it's your mother's dutch-apple pie, chocolate-chip cookies, or jamoca-almond-fudge ice cream. Focus on that treat for a moment.

What happened? You forgot all about slithering snakes—until I mentioned them again. What's the point? Our minds will be filled with something—either good or evil. By adopting pure thoughts, we can push out impure thoughts. Philippians 4:8 identifies the kind of thoughts God has in mind for us:

WHATEVER IS TRUE, WHATEVER IS HONORABLE, WHATEVER IS JUST, WHATEVER IS PURE, WHATEVER IS LOVELY, WHATEVER IS COMMENDABLE—IF THERE IS ANY MORAL EXCELLENCE AND IF THERE IS ANY PRAISE—DWELL ON THESE THINGS. *PHILIPPIANS 4:8*

"Dwell on these things" when the poison of lust and ungodly thoughts begins to enter your mind. The more you fill your mind with purity and the less with impurity, the greater your ability to maintain Christlike purity and resist temptation. When the wrong thoughts come, replace them with God's truth:

WE TAKE CAPTIVE EVERY THOUGHT TO MAKE IT OBEDIENT TO CHRIST. *2 CORINTHIANS 10:5, NIV*

As we establish healthy boundaries, stop feeding our desires, and guard our hearts, we begin to master lust. In time its demands become less pressing and more manageable.

Identify a desire or a practice you need to overcome.

_____

Set a boundary that will help you avoid it.

_____

Name something you will do to replace
impure thoughts with pure ones.

_____

_____

THE DAY IN REVIEW

Review today's lesson.
What was the most important concept you read today?

_____

_____

How will this truth challenge you to be like Christ?

_____

_____

_____

Ask God to help you set healthy boundaries, guard your heart,
and replace impure thoughts with pure ones.
Ask Him to help you implement the actions you identified
at the end of today's lesson. Write your prayer below.

_____

_____

_____

_____

_____

_____

_____

_____

Wise Strategies

day 3

For the rest of the week we will look at six strategies to gain victory over sexual temptation. We will consider the first two strategies today.

Imagine that someone's weakness is eating doughnuts. Told by his doctor that he must quit, he vows to God, "No more doughnuts." He promises his family, "No more doughnuts." He prays and calls the church to add him to the prayer chain.

But then this guy keeps reading about doughnuts, listening to doughnut music, and watching television programs about making doughnuts. He spends his time with other doughnut lovers talking about doughnuts. He jokes about doughnuts at the office, where he often glances at the doughnut calendars on the wall. He subscribes to *Doughnut Desires*, losing himself in its glossy color photos.

Before long he's driving the long way to work that just happens to take him by a doughnut shop. He rolls down the window and inhales. Pretty soon he's buying the morning newspaper from the rack outside the doughnut shop. He lingers just long enough to examine the doughnuts through the window.

Then he remembers that he has to make a phone call, and what do you know? The doughnut shop has a pay phone. And since he's there anyway, why not have a cup of coffee?

Are you surprised when this man inevitably gives in, breaks his vow, and eats doughnuts?

This man wisely established several levels of accountability. He went directly to God and asked others to intercede for him. He told his family. If he had stopped his activity there, he would've been OK. Unfortunately, he didn't change his behavior and stop his unhealthy habits.

How do you think this story applies to our study of purity?

_____

_____

If we learn nothing else from the parable of the doughnuts, we should learn that sincere intentions—and even prayers—are not enough. To have victory over temptation, we must have clear goals and sound strategies, and we must carry them out diligently.

What is our first line of defense against impurity? We find the answer in the Apostle Paul's first letter to the church in the sex-saturated city of Corinth:

FLEE FROM SEXUAL IMMORALITY! *1 CORINTHIANS 6:18*

When it comes to sexual temptation, it pays to be a coward. He who hesitates—and rationalizes—is lost. He who runs, lives. The first strategy for overcoming sexual temptation is to run from it. When temptation comes, keep walking in the right direction. Don't ogle, peer, or even glance. Get outta there!

One young man who employed this strategy was Joseph. Sold into slavery by his brothers, Joseph found favor with Potiphar, an officer of Pharaoh and the captain of the guard (see Gen. 37). Potiphar put Joseph in charge of the household, and Joseph managed everything Potiphar owned. Then one day Potiphar's wife asked Joseph to sleep with her (see Gen. 39:7). Joseph's handsome frame had gotten the attention of his master's wife. But he wasn't just good-looking. He had great wisdom, far beyond his years. What was Joseph's reply?

HE REFUSED AND SAID TO HIS MASTER'S WIFE, "LOOK, MY MASTER DOES NOT CONCERN HIMSELF WITH ANYTHING IN HIS HOUSE, AND HE HAS PUT ALL THAT HE OWNS UNDER MY AUTHORITY. NO ONE IN THIS HOUSE IS GREATER THAN I AM. HE HAS WITHHELD NOTHING FROM ME EXCEPT YOU, BECAUSE YOU ARE HIS WIFE. SO HOW COULD I DO SUCH A GREAT EVIL AND SIN AGAINST GOD?" *GENESIS 39:8-9*

But Mrs. Potiphar didn't take no for an answer.

ALTHOUGH SHE SPOKE TO JOSEPH DAY AFTER DAY, HE REFUSED TO GO TO BED
WITH HER. SHE GRABBED HIM BY HIS GARMENT AND SAID, "SLEEP WITH ME!"
BUT LEAVING HIS GARMENT IN HER HAND, HE ESCAPED AND RAN OUTSIDE.
GENESIS 39:10,12

When Potiphar's wife finally pushed herself on Joseph, he ran,
knowing it would be "a great evil and sin against God." Don't
stay and try to resist temptation when you can run from it.

The second strategy for overcoming temptation is to keep
your distance. If you told your children, "Don't play on the
freeway," what would you expect of them? To go down by the
freeway, sidle up to the edge, climb on the guardrail, dangle
their legs out, or dance along the white line on the shoulder
of the road? Obviously not. That's flirting with disaster. "But
we didn't go on the freeway," they might protest. Maybe not.
But if they keep trying to discover how close they can get, it's
only a matter of time until they get run over.

The question "How far can we go?" really means "How close
can we get without actually sinning? Tell us where the line is so
that we can inch our toes right up to the edge." That's not how
God operates. His Word says,

FLEE FROM YOUTHFUL PASSIONS, AND PURSUE RIGHTEOUSNESS, FAITH, LOVE,
AND PEACE, ALONG WITH THOSE WHO CALL ON THE LORD FROM A PURE HEART.
2 TIMOTHY 2:22

When you're fleeing, you don't keep turning around and asking,
"Is this far enough?" A spirit of obedience says, "If my Father
tells me this is wrong, I'll stay away from it. Period."

What are the first two strategies
for victory over sexual temptation?

1. _____ 2. _____

What do you need to flee from?

_____

What do you need to keep your distance from?

_____

When you flee from something, you go toward
something else. Read 2 Timothy 2:22 again (p. 59)
and name something you especially need to pursue.

_____

THE DAY IN REVIEW

Review today's lesson.
What was the most important concept you read today?

_____

How will this truth challenge you to be like Christ?

_____
_____

Ask God to help you flee from and keep your distance from
the impurity you identified at the end of today's lesson. Ask
Him to help you pursue righteousness, faith, love, and peace
as He develops a pure heart in you. Write your prayer below.

_____
_____
_____
_____
_____
_____

An Ounce of Prevention

day 4

We are in the process of learning six strategies for defeating sexual temptation. Yesterday you learned the first two strategies.

Write the first two strategies here.

1. _____

2. _____

Today we will look at three more strategies. The first is to antici-pate and prevent temptation.

People whose jobs require travel are often confronted with sexual temptation. Home, family, and community, which provide natural restraints, are left behind. The anonymity, loneliness, and leisuretime that sometimes come with travel can spell catastrophe. Many godly men and women travel with complete moral victory, but many others have long track records of failure. The best solu-tion for them is to stop traveling, even if it means finding another job that pays less.

At a men's conference I once asked those who travel to share guidelines for resisting sexual temptation. One man said that for years he had watched immoral movies in hotel rooms. After repeated failures he finally decided to do something drastic. Now when he checks into a hotel, he asks for the TV to be removed from his room. Although the staff may question him, he politely insists, and he has never been refused. Now immorality is no longer just a button push away. This man's actions say, "I'm serious about this, Lord."

This man discovered a great principle: it's always easier to anticipate and prevent temptation than to resist it. We can make decisions in moments of strength that will prevent temptation in moments of weakness.

Do you remember the Purity Principle? Write it here.

_____

What is smart about anticipating and preventing temptation toward sexual impurity?

What is stupid about not doing so?

Name a way you can anticipate and prevent a temptation that often comes your way. _____

The fourth strategy for overcoming sexual temptation is to cultivate your inner spiritual life. This study does not advocate behavior modification. Simple guidelines and the exhortation to try harder aren't enough to break the grip of lust or the power of deeply ingrained habits. There is no easy formula for remaining pure. Self-reformation may bring limited benefits, but it leads to self-righteousness. The Christian life is more than sin management. It is divine transformation and enablement to live righteously. This kind of change is possible only through the indwelling power of the risen Christ.

How does a believer access Christ's power?

Ultimately, the battle for purity is won or lost in quietness, on our knees with God and in collaboration with our fellow soldiers. Busyness wears down our ability to hear the prompt-ings of God's Spirit, His Word, and His people. Fatigue makes us oblivious to the process by which we consume harmful thoughts. Healthy self-examination reveals to us our triggers— the situations that tempt us. We then take these to God.

Time with God is the fountain from which holiness flows ... and joy and delight. Time with God reminds us who we are— and whose we are. When we daily set our minds on heaven, where Christ is, He empowers us to put to death the works of the old nature—including sexual immorality, impurity, and lust.

**Identify at least one action you will take to cultivate
your inner spiritual life.**
❏ Read and meditate on Scripture.
❏ Schedule time to slow down and listen to God.
❏ Have a daily time of prayer.
❏ Other: _____

Let's consider one more strategy today that can help us resist
and overcome sexual temptation: memorize and quote Scripture.
When we are tempted, we can follow the example of Jesus, who
quoted Scripture to answer Satan's temptations.

**Read Matthew 4:2-11. Draw lines across the columns
to match Jesus' scriptural answers to Satan's temptations.**

Satan's Temptation	Jesus' Answer
"If You are the Son of God, tell these stones to become bread" (v. 4).	"Worship the Lord your God, and serve only Him" (v. 10; see Deut. 6:13).
"If You are the Son of God, throw Yourself down. For it is written: 'He will give His angels orders concerning you' and 'they will support you with their hands so that you will not strike your foot against a stone'" (v. 6; see Ps. 91:11-12).	"Man must not live on bread alone but on every word that comes from the mouth of God" (v. 4; see Deut. 8:3).
"I will give You all these things if You will fall down and worship me" (v. 9).	"Do not test the Lord your God" (v. 7; see Deut. 6:16).

Follow Jesus' example and heed the psalmist's words when Satan tries to attack your sexual purity:

I HAVE TREASURED YOUR WORD IN MY HEART
SO THAT I MAY NOT SIN AGAINST YOU. *PSALM 119:11*

**This study contains many Scripture passages.
Choose several that you find helpful and transfer them
to cards, your personal digital assistant, or another source
that will remind you to read and memorize them.**

When you are tempted, use God's Word to fight back. The Bible gives you the words to say. Have them ready by storing them in your mind and heart.

THE DAY IN REVIEW

**Review today's lesson.
What was the most important concept you read today?**

_____

How will this truth challenge you to be like Christ?

_____

**Review any commitments you made in today's study and pray
that God will help you anticipate and prevent sexual temptation,
cultivate your inner life, and memorize Scripture to quote
when temptation arises. Write your prayer below.**

_____
_____
_____
_____

Don't Give Up

Jesus taught His disciples that they should "always pray and not give up" (Luke 18:1, NIV). Then he told them a parable. Although Jesus told this story about persistence to emphasize God's willingness to grant justice, think of it in terms of going before God with your request to be sexually pure. Amazing thing about God: He never tires of our asking for His help.

THERE WAS A JUDGE IN ONE TOWN WHO DIDN'T FEAR GOD OR RESPECT MAN. AND A WIDOW IN THAT TOWN KEPT COMING TO HIM, SAYING, "GIVE ME JUSTICE AGAINST MY ADVERSARY."

FOR A WHILE HE WAS UNWILLING, BUT LATER HE SAID TO HIMSELF, "EVEN THOUGH I DON'T FEAR GOD OR RESPECT MAN, YET BECAUSE THIS WIDOW KEEPS PESTERING ME, I WILL GIVE HER JUSTICE, SO SHE DOESN'T WEAR ME OUT BY HER PERSISTENT COMING." *LUKE 18:2-5*

What quality caused the judge to give the widow justice?

_____

Our final strategy for overcoming sexual temptation is not to give up. We are often brought to our knees after losing a battle. But we need to fall to our knees before the battle begins. Too often we declare a truce with sin, allowing it to claim more territory in our lives and in our homes.

Have you declared a truce with a certain sin?   ❑ Yes   ❑ No

Jesus says: "Don't give up! Pray for God's help." You may be suspicious if you've ever heard "Just read the Bible and pray, and that will solve everything." No, it won't solve everything, but nothing will be solved without it. Jesus knew what He was talking about. So did James:

SUBMIT TO GOD. BUT RESIST THE DEVIL, AND HE WILL FLEE FROM YOU. DRAW NEAR TO GOD, AND HE WILL DRAW NEAR TO YOU. *JAMES 4:7-8*

> **If we resist the Devil, he will _____ from us. If we submit and draw near to God, He will _____ _____ to us.**

The closer we get to God, the farther away we are from the Devil. God doesn't leave us to handle our temptations alone. He is far more powerful than Satan. And His Son, Jesus, is uniquely qualified to help us when we are tempted:

HE MADE THE ONE WHO DID NOT KNOW SIN TO BE SIN FOR US, SO THAT WE MIGHT BECOME THE RIGHTEOUSNESS OF GOD IN HIM. *2 CORINTHIANS 5:21*
SINCE HE HIMSELF [JESUS] WAS TESTED AND HAS SUFFERED, HE IS ABLE TO HELP THOSE WHO ARE TESTED. *HEBREWS 2:18*

> **How is Jesus able to help us when we are tempted?**
> _____

How incredible is that? Although Jesus was sinless, He experienced sin for us. And because He experienced temptation, He offers strength to face—and resist—any temptation if we ask Him to help us.

Many people have been defeated so long that they've given up, guaranteeing that they'll keep losing.

> **Have you given up on resisting a certain sin?**
> ❏ Yes ❏ No

Would God tell you to abstain from impurity if that were impossible? No! God calls us and empowers us to be overcomers—those who experience victory over sin.

An overcomer told me, "People never change until it hurts them less to change than to stay the same." Tens of thousands of people—most of whom had to become desperate first—are living proof that victory over sexual temptation is possible.

Think of your greatest sexual temptation. Mark the continuum to indicate the degree to which you want victory.

I've given up.   I'm fighting.   I'm desperate for victory.

If someone put a gun to your head and said he would pull the trigger if you looked at pornography, would you do it? No? Then you don't have to. Period. You can turn it off, walk out, or shut your eyes. You don't have to click on that link. You don't have to fondle that person or allow him or her to fondle you. The alternative is to draw on supernatural resources.

In the following verses underline evidence that God's supernatural power helps you with anything you need.

HIS DIVINE POWER HAS GIVEN US EVERYTHING REQUIRED FOR LIFE AND GODLINESS, THROUGH THE KNOWLEDGE OF HIM WHO CALLED US BY HIS OWN GLORY AND GOODNESS. BY THESE HE HAS GIVEN US VERY GREAT AND PRECIOUS PROMISES, SO THAT THROUGH THEM YOU MAY SHARE IN THE DIVINE NATURE, ESCAPING THE CORRUPTION THAT IS IN THE WORLD BECAUSE OF EVIL DESIRES. *2 PETER 1:3-4*

THE GRACE OF GOD HAS APPEARED, WITH SALVATION FOR ALL PEOPLE, INSTRUCTING US TO DENY GODLESSNESS AND WORLDLY LUSTS AND TO LIVE IN A SENSIBLE, RIGHTEOUS, AND GODLY WAY IN THE PRESENT AGE. *TITUS 2:11-12*

The same grace that brings salvation teaches us to say no to the things of the world. It also teaches us to live self-controlled, upright, and godly lives.

Check the benefits of grace, according to these verses.
- ❏ Offers salvation to everyone
- ❏ Instructs us to deny godlessness and worldly lusts
- ❏ Allows us to enjoy the lusts of the flesh
- ❏ Instructs us to live in a sensible, righteous, and godly way

Our sexual struggles remind us of our need for grace and empowerment—and make us long for our ultimate redemption.

If a lifetime of purity seems inconceivable, commit yourself in 24-hour increments. Get help. Be wise. Avoid temptation. Go to Christ. Experience His sufficiency. Draw on His supernatural power. When the first 24 hours are over and you've seen that the Lord is good, commit to the next 24 hours. Depend on Him one day at a time.

Never underestimate Christ. Sin is not more powerful than God. Don't imagine that victory is reserved only for heaven. God says otherwise. We are not to wait for victory. We are to live in it now:

WHATEVER HAS BEEN BORN OF GOD CONQUERS THE WORLD. *1 JOHN 5:4*

Conquering the world. Sound good? We can do it as we draw strength from Christ.

Check some things you are willing to do to win the fight against sexual temptation.
- ❏ Persistently pray and ask for God's help.
- ❏ Ask for and depend on the power of the Holy Spirit.
- ❏ Actively resist the Devil.
- ❏ Draw near to God through Christian disciplines and worship.
- ❏ Ask for prayer and counsel from Christians to whom you are accountable.
- ❏ Implement the strategies you have studied this week.

Review this week's study by writing the six strategies
for gaining victory over sexual temptation.

1. _____
2. _____
3. _____
4. _____
5. _____
6. _____

THE DAY IN REVIEW

Review today's lesson.
What was the most important concept you read today?

_____
_____
_____

How will this truth challenge you to be like Christ?

_____
_____
_____

Ask God to help you implement the strategies you have
studied and the commitments you have made this week to
overcome sexual temptation. Ask Him to help you remember
that you can overcome the world! Write your prayer below.

_____
_____
_____
_____
_____
_____
_____
_____
_____
_____

week 4

Getting Personal

A Radical Approach

Suppose I said to you: "There's a great-looking girl down the street. Let's go look through her window and watch her undress, then pose for us naked from the waist up. Then she and her boyfriend will get in a car and have sex. Let's listen and watch the windows steam up!"

You'd be shocked. You'd think, *What a pervert!*

But suppose I said: "Hey, come on over. Let's watch *Titanic.*"

Christians recommend this movie, church youth groups view it together, and many believers watch it in their homes. Yet the movie contains precisely the scenes I described. So our young men lust after the girl on the screen, and our young women learn how to get a man's attention.

How does something shocking and shameful somehow become acceptable because we watch it through a television instead of a window? In terms of the lasting effects on our minds and morals, what's the difference? Each day Christians across the country, including many church leaders, watch people undress through the window of television. We peek on people committing fornication and adultery—acts that God calls an abomination:

YOU ARE TO KEEP MY STATUTES AND ORDINANCES. YOU MUST NOT COMMIT
ANY OF THESE ABOMINATIONS. *LEVITICUS 18:26*

"These abominations" refers to the sexual sins being committed
by the Egyptians and the Canaanites (see Lev. 18:6-18). God
warned His people not to repeat those behaviors.

The enemy's strategy is to normalize evil. Consider young
people who struggle with homosexual temptation. What's the
effect on them when they watch television shows in which
homosexual partners live together in apparent normality? Parents
who wouldn't dream of letting a dirty-minded adult baby-sit
their children do it every time they let their kids surf the channels.

In our culture it's easy for parents and children to become
desensitized to immorality. Why are we surprised when our son
gets a girl pregnant if we've allowed him to watch hundreds of
immoral acts and hear thousands of sexual innuendos? "But it's
just one little sex scene." Suppose I offered you a cookie, saying:
"A few mouse droppings fell into the batter, but for the most
part it's a great cookie. You won't even notice." Proverbs says,

TO FEAR THE LORD IS TO HATE EVIL. *PROVERBS 8:13*

**Write the words *God* and *evil* on opposite ends
of the line to represent their opposing natures.
Then draw a thick barrier between them.**

God and evil are diametrically opposed. How can we hate evil
when we are being entertained by it? How can we be pure when
we amuse ourselves with impurity? They're like oil and water;
they don't mix.

Consider Christ's words:

IF YOUR RIGHT EYE CAUSES YOU TO SIN, GOUGE IT OUT AND THROW IT AWAY.
FOR IT IS BETTER THAT YOU LOSE ONE OF THE PARTS OF YOUR BODY THAN
FOR YOUR WHOLE BODY TO BE THROWN INTO HELL. AND IF YOUR RIGHT
HAND CAUSES YOU TO SIN, CUT IT OFF AND THROW IT AWAY. FOR IT IS BETTER
THAT YOU LOSE ONE OF THE PARTS OF YOUR BODY THAN FOR YOUR WHOLE
BODY TO GO INTO HELL! *MATTHEW 5:27-30*

Why do you think Jesus painted such a shocking picture?

_____

I believe that Jesus wants us to take radical steps—to do whatever
is necessary—to deal with sexual temptation. The hand and eye
are not the causes of sin. A blind man can still lust, while a man
without a hand can steal. But the eye is a means of accessing both
godly and ungodly input. And the hand is a means of performing
righteous or sinful acts. So we must govern what the eye looks
at and what the hand does.

To take Jesus seriously, we must think radically about
sexual purity.

In the following examples, draw lines across the columns to make the radical choice in each situation.

You can't keep your eyes away from explicit images in videos.	Turn off the radio.
Your thoughts trip you up when you're with a certain person.	Don't go to video stores.
A certain kind of music charges you up erotically.	Block 900 numbers from your phone.
You make phone calls you shouldn't.	Stop attending or watching sports events.
You are tempted by cheerleaders at sports events.	Stop hanging out with that person.

Identify a radical action you need to take in regard to sexual temptation.

_____

Romans 13:14 instructs us to "make no plans to satisfy the fleshly desires." We must stay away from people, places, and contexts that make sin more likely.

Where are you most likely to be tempted?

_____

Whether it's the lingerie department, the swimming pool, or the athletic club, if it trips you up, stay away from it! If it's certain bookstores, hangouts, or old friends, stay away from them. If cable or satellite TV, network TV, the Internet, or computers are your problem, get rid of them. Say no to whatever is pulling you away from Jesus. Remember, if you want a different outcome, you must make different choices.

If you are falling, get rid of what's tripping you up. Think that's radical? It's nothing compared to what Jesus said: "If it would keep you from sexual temptation, you'd be better off poking out your eye and cutting off your hand." Now *that's* radical!

Many claim that they're serious about purity, but then they say, "No way; I will not give up cable TV" or "I won't give my wife my computer password." Followers of Jesus have endured torture and have given their lives in obedience to Him. And we're whining about giving up cable TV?

Name anything you are struggling to give up. _____

If you are Jesus' disciple, you can take His words to heart:

IF ANYONE WANTS TO COME WITH ME, HE MUST DENY HIMSELF, TAKE UP HIS CROSS, AND FOLLOW ME. *MATTHEW 16:24*

When Jesus called us to take up our crosses and follow Him, He meant sacrifices greater than forgoing Internet access.

Start thinking about the following questions.
They are rhetorical questions for now.
I'll ask you to respond to them personally in day 5.
- How sold out are you to the battle for purity?
- How desperate are you to have victory over sin?
- How radical are you willing to get for your Lord?
- How much do you want the joy and peace that can be found only in God?

Purity comes only to those who truly want it.

THE DAY IN REVIEW

Review today's lesson.
What was the most important concept you read today?

_____

How will this truth challenge you to be like Christ?

_____

_____

Ask God to help you take your relationship with Him
seriously and be willing to take the radical measures
you identified in this lesson in order to be sexually pure.
Write your prayer below.

_____

_____

_____

_____

_____

_____

_____

Guidelines for Singles

day 2

A large percentage of today's population is single. This group includes young people, adults who have never married, and those who became single through death or divorce.

For young singles, the unprecedented combination of leisuretime, money, and transportation is historically unique. Add to this the lack of parental supervision and the large gap between the average age of puberty and marriage. Mix in the media's saturation with sex and their portrayal of premarital sex as normal. The result is overwhelming temptation.

If you aren't single or haven't been single for a long time, don't skip this day's study. You know people who are single. Step into their shoes and look at sexual purity through their eyes.

If you are married, write the names of several single adults you know. Keep them in mind as you study today.

_____

_____

Single Christians must adopt wise biblical strategies to live righteously. One guideline God calls them to exercise is self-control, a fruit of the Spirit:

THE FRUIT OF THE SPIRIT IS LOVE, JOY, PEACE, PATIENCE, KINDNESS, GOODNESS, FAITH, GENTLENESS, SELF-CONTROL. AGAINST SUCH THINGS THERE IS NO LAW. *GALATIANS 5:22-23*

Self-control is essential for Christian singles. God made sex drives. When stimulated, those drives move toward a climax. This is a simple fact of biology. Caressing each other in sexually stimulating ways is foreplay. And God has designed foreplay to culminate in sexual intercourse. Logically, then, because intercourse is forbidden outside marriage, so is foreplay. Because sexual intercourse before marriage is wrong, it is also wrong to engage in activity that propels mind and body toward it.

Therefore, the line must be drawn before either person becomes sexually stimulated. Forbid fondling and other actions that turn you on. Once you let your body cross the line, it will neither know nor care about your Christian convictions. Men are more quickly and easily stimulated than women. A woman often thinks extended kisses and hugs are fine, but these sexually stimulate a man, and he is tempted to push for more. You must draw the line far enough back that neither of you crosses it.

If one of you begins to be stimulated even by apparently innocent physical contact, both of you should back off immediately. If you don't, you're choosing to stay in a canoe headed toward a waterfall. Those who engage in sexual stimulation should not be surprised when they finally have intercourse. It's the natural, predictable result of the choices they've made. If you want a different outcome, you have to make different choices.

Singles also face sexual temptation when they maintain harmful social relationships. Scripture says that we are influenced by the people we hang around with:

BAD COMPANY CORRUPTS GOOD MORALS. *1 CORINTHIANS 15:33*

By nature we are influenced by our surroundings. When we place ourselves in a godly atmosphere with godly people, we are influenced toward godliness. When we place ourselves in an ungodly atmosphere with ungodly people, we are influenced toward ungodliness:

THE ONE WHO WALKS WITH THE WISE WILL BECOME WISE,
BUT A COMPANION OF FOOLS WILL SUFFER HARM. *PROVERBS 13:20*

We become like the people we spend time with:

PEOPLE WILL BE LOVERS OF SELF, LOVERS OF MONEY, BOASTFUL, PROUD, BLASPHEMERS, DISOBEDIENT TO PARENTS, UNGRATEFUL, UNHOLY, UNLOVING, IRRECONCILABLE, SLANDERERS, WITHOUT SELF-CONTROL, BRUTAL, WITHOUT LOVE FOR WHAT IS GOOD, TRAITORS, RECKLESS, CONCEITED, LOVERS OF PLEASURE RATHER THAN LOVERS OF GOD, HOLDING TO THE FORM OF RELIGION BUT DENYING ITS POWER. AVOID THESE PEOPLE! *2 TIMOTHY 3:2-5*

What does Paul tell us to do? _____ these people.

That's the same word he uses when addressing sexual immorality and temptation. Avoid them!

If you date, you may find the following guidelines helpful.

1. If you're a Christian, date only Christians:

DO NOT BE MISMATCHED WITH UNBELIEVERS. FOR WHAT PARTNERSHIP IS THERE BETWEEN RIGHTEOUSNESS AND LAWLESSNESS? OR WHAT FELLOWSHIP DOES LIGHT HAVE WITH DARKNESS? *2 CORINTHIANS 6:14*

Complete these equations:

_____ = light.

_____ = darkness.

2. If you're a committed disciple, date only committed disciples. Remember that Christ is with you all evening—wherever you go and in whatever you do. Remember that your date is your Christian brother or sister, not your lover.
3. Go out in groups, not alone. Much sexual temptation is generated by our social custom of coupling and isolating young people. This stands in stark contrast to the Hebrew

culture and other cultures, which require that young single people spend time together only when adults are present. You can enjoy fun, positive friendships with persons of the opposite sex and can be involved in a variety of activities without pairing with one person.

4. Focus on talk, not touch; conversation, not contact.
5. Avoid fast-moving relationships or instant intimacy.
6. Plan the entire evening in advance, with no gaps in time or activities.
7. Avoid setups. Never be alone—on a couch; in a car late at night; or in a house, especially in a bedroom.
8. Be accountable to someone about your purity.

If you are single, to whom are you accountable? _____
Do you tell them where you will be on a date? ❏ Yes ❏ No
Have they met the person you want to date? ❏ Yes ❏ No
If you are married, would you volunteer to be someone to whom a single person can be accountable? ❏ Yes ❏ No

9. Imagine that your parents and church leaders are watching you through the window. Realize that God is watching. He has said:

MY GAZE TAKES IN ALL THEIR WAYS. THEY ARE NOT CONCEALED FROM ME, AND THEIR GUILT IS NOT HIDDEN FROM MY SIGHT. *JEREMIAH 16:17*

10. Write down your standards and enforce them yourself. Never depend on someone else to enforce them.
11. Don't do anything with your date that you wouldn't want someone else to do with your future mate.
12. Beware of the moral degeneration that can occur in long dating relationships and long engagements. Once you and your parents agree on marriage, it's dangerous to wait longer than necessary:

I SAY TO THE UNMARRIED AND TO WIDOWS: IT IS GOOD FOR THEM IF THEY REMAIN AS I AM. BUT IF THEY DO NOT HAVE SELF-CONTROL, THEY SHOULD MARRY, FOR IT IS BETTER TO MARRY THAN TO BURN WITH DESIRE. *1 CORINTHIANS 7:8-9*

If you are single, go back and check the guidelines you are following now. Place an X beside the guidelines you are not following. Circle the numbers of those that you will commit to implement in your dating life.

THE DAY IN REVIEW

Review today's lesson.
What was the most important concept you read today?

_____

_____

How will this truth challenge you to be like Christ?

_____

_____

If you are single, ask God to help you follow the road to sexual purity. Write your prayer below.
If you aren't single, refer to the single adults' names you wrote at the beginning of today's lesson. Pray that God will strengthen these singles and keep them sexually pure. Tell them that you are praying for them. Write your prayer below.

_____

_____

_____

_____

_____

_____

Guidelines for Couples

day 3

Today and tomorrow we will look at ways married adults can maintain purity. If you are single, don't pass over this study. As you study, think of married couples you know. You may be in their position someday. Try to see the challenges of purity from their perspective.

Name some couples you will keep in mind as you study.

Countless marriages have been destroyed when casual relationships turned into infatuation. A relationship can be inappropriate long before it becomes erotic, so we must spot moral danger early. Today we will examine three principles to help married couples maintain a pure relationship.

The first principle is to cultivate and guard your marriage. You can do this in several ways.

1. Regularly evaluate your relationship with your mate, watching for the red flags of discontentment and a deteriorating relationship. Talk openly. Work through the issues you discover, even if the process is painful.

2. Be sensitive to your spouse's sexual needs. Remember that marriage involves a sexual responsibility:

DO NOT DEPRIVE ONE ANOTHER—EXCEPT WHEN YOU AGREE, FOR A TIME, TO DEVOTE YOURSELVES TO PRAYER. THEN COME TOGETHER AGAIN; OTHERWISE, SATAN MAY TEMPT YOU BECAUSE OF YOUR LACK OF SELF-CONTROL. *1 CORINTHIANS 7:5*

Who decides to stop having sexual relations for a time?
❏ Husband   ❏ Wife   ❏ Husband and wife in agreement

Paul said that when a couple forgo sex, they are to agree on a time. Communicate honestly about your needs. Don't harbor resentment. If one of you feels that you need sex more or less often, set specific times so that neither of you has to wonder when it's the right time.

3. Date your spouse. Put it on your schedule. Dating doesn't end with the wedding ceremony.

4. At work surround yourself with reminders of your spouse and children with photographs, artwork, and special gifts. If you travel on business, take with you a photo of your spouse and/or children. Call home frequently. If you have a laptop computer, put your favorite family photo on the desktop.

5. Be fiercely loyal to your spouse. Speak highly of him or her. Don't share marriage problems with someone of the opposite sex unless the person is a family member or a professional counselor. Even then be careful and discerning.

6. Pray with and for each other. All believers are to pray for one another, but praying for a spouse is a special privilege and responsibility. Share your prayer needs with your spouse; don't wait for your spouse to ask. How can he or she pray for you unless you share your needs?

**What specific needs does your spouse have today
that you can pray for?**

_____

**If you can't answer this question, talk with your spouse
to discover these needs. Then be faithful to pray for him or her.**

7. Work hard to bring your spouse into your world. Talk about your job, projects, struggles, disappointments, concerns, priorities, and values. Listen to each other. This means putting down the newspaper, magazine, or mail; turning off the TV; and getting away from the computer. Don't live two separate lives under one roof. This is the first step toward an affair with "someone who understands me and my world."

Christian married couples face the same heartaches, struggles, and frustrations as other couples. When our marriages become plagued by resentment, boredom, or hurt, we become vulnerable to Satan's lie about the intrigue and excitement of a new person. Remember that we have supernatural resources to deal with our problems. The answer is not finding a new person but finding a fresh appreciation of the old person.

Review the seven ideas for cultivating and guarding your marriage. Write down two that you will commit to work on, along with specific actions you will take.

1. _____

2. _____

The second principle for maintaining purity in marriage is to rekindle attraction to your mate. A friend admitted that he was no longer attracted to his wife. He committed himself to praying daily that God would make her the most attractive woman in the world to him. Within a month that prayer was answered decisively. She didn't change. He did. Their marriage was revitalized. Here are some ways to rekindle attraction.

1. Choose to be captivated by your spouse.

DRINK WATER FROM YOUR OWN CISTERN,
WATER FLOWING FROM YOUR OWN WELL.
SHOULD YOUR SPRINGS FLOW IN THE STREETS,
STREAMS OF WATER IN THE PUBLIC SQUARES?
THEY SHOULD BE FOR YOU ALONE
AND NOT FOR YOU [TO SHARE] WITH STRANGERS.
LET YOUR FOUNTAIN BE BLESSED,
AND TAKE PLEASURE IN THE WIFE OF YOUR YOUTH.
A LOVING DOE, A GRACEFUL FAWN—
LET HER BREASTS ALWAYS SATISFY YOU;
BE LOST IN HER LOVE FOREVER. *PROVERBS 5:15-19*

What does it means to drink water from your own well?

_____

**What does the phrase "be lost in her love forever"
mean to you?**

_____

Problems will come in every marriage. But do everything you can to enjoy your spouse and your marriage. The friend who shared with me that he was no longer attracted to his wife didn't tell her that. He accepted the responsibility to pray that he, not she, would change.

2. Treasure your marriage partner. Restrict your eyes to your mate, and he or she will become the true desire of your heart. You'll be lost in his or her love forever. This is what Proverbs 15:15-16 is talking about.

3. Train your eyes to turn away from stimulating images and fix them on your spouse. When your sex drive is activated, lock it on your partner. What we focus on shapes our desires. By denying errant appetites and meditating on the right things, you can train yourself to desire what is proper.

4. Take care of your physical health. Be as attractive to your mate as you can. Be modest with others in public and sexy with your spouse in private—never the opposite!

5. Get help when needed. Sometimes marriage problems need outside assistance. If this is true of you, get help immediately. Talk to your pastor or have him refer you to a Christian counselor who specializes in marriage relationships.

6. Use Christian books and discipleship resources to enrich your marriage. Wonderful Christian marriage conferences have rescued and revived countless marriages.[1]

**Place a ✔ beside each action that you currently practice.
Place an X beside those that you are not doing.**

❏ Choose to be captivated by your spouse.

❏ Treasure your marriage partner.

❏ Train your eyes to turn away from stimulating images and fix them on your spouse.
❏ Take care of your physical health.
❏ Get help when needed.
❏ Use Christian resources to enrich your marriage.

Underline one guideline you will commit to work on.

THE DAY IN REVIEW

Review today's lesson.
What was the most important concept you read today?

_____

How will this truth challenge you to be like Christ?

_____

_____

If you are married, review the commitments you made today. Ask God to help you cultivate and guard your marriage and rekindle attraction to your spouse. Write your prayer below. If you are single, think about the married couples you named at the beginning of today's lesson. Pray that they will submit to God's ideal of purity. Ask Him to strengthen their relationships. Write your prayer below.

_____

_____

_____

_____

_____

_____

_____

[1]For information about LifeWay marriage-enrichment events, visit *www.lifeway.com/events* or call (800) 254-2022.

More Guidelines for Couples

Yesterday you learned two principles for maintaining purity
in marriage.

day 4

Write the principles you learned yesterday.

1. _____
2. _____

Today you will learn two more principles for married couples.
The first one is to be honest with your mate. Every adulterous
relationship begins with deception, and most deception begins
with seemingly innocent secrets.

Check any secrets you have kept from your spouse.
- ❏ Internet sites you've visited ❏ Movies you've seen
- ❏ How you've spent money ❏ How you've spent time
- ❏ Other: _____

As innocent as a secret seems, it is deceit. Lust thrives on secrecy.
    Nothing defuses a secret like exposure. Honest communica-
tion between husband and wife will make them allies, not
adversaries. Although discussing sexual temptation initially
causes pain, it also produces relief and growth.

CONFESS YOUR SINS TO ONE ANOTHER AND PRAY FOR ONE ANOTHER,
SO THAT YOU MAY BE HEALED. *JAMES 5:16*

What are the two requirements in this verse?
1. _____ 2. _____

Although your spouse may be unaware of your sin, she has been
deeply affected by it. If you don't confess it, you cheat her twice:

85

first by committing the sin itself and second by not allowing her to forgive you or respond as she chooses.

Husbands, be honest with your wives about your sexual struggles. Wives, ask your husband about his temptations. Encourage him to be open with you and ask him how you can help him remain honest and accountable. Don't be naive about the battles in male minds. For example, don't recommend that he and your best friend jog together. If you've agreed that he should use the Internet only when you are nearby, don't think, *I'm going to bed; he will be fine.* Don't discourage his openness by acting superior because he struggles in ways you don't. Be honest with him about your sexual secrets. Have you fantasized about men, read steamy romance novels, viewed inappropriate chick flicks, or indulged in gossip or slander? Confess your sins to him. He needs you as a friend and an ally, not an adversary.

**Have you been honest with your spouse about
your sexual temptations and struggles?** ❑ Yes ❑ No
Do you have anything to confess to him or her? ❑ Yes ❑ No
If so, schedule a time to talk and pray together.

The final principle for married couples is to teach biblical concepts of purity to your children. Christian parents have an obligation to the Lord to rear their children to be pure. Sometimes our children may fail to listen to us, but rarely will they fail to imitate us. Let's look at some guidelines for giving our children a legacy of purity.
1. Show children a loving, affectionate, and pure marriage.
2. Train children in choice and consequence, wisdom and foolishness, as exemplified in Proverbs. Teach them to love righteousness and to hate sin. In week 2 we learned that our sins can affect our children and several generations to come. Your great-great-grandchildren could live with the effects of your sinful behavior. Stop the sin at your generation!
3. Teach children self-control. The ability to say no in other areas will carry over to sexual purity. Self-control is a fruit

of the Spirit (see Gal. 5:23). Our children cannot inherit the fruit of the Holy Spirit, but they can learn how to develop godly self-control.

4. Exercise gracious but firm control over children's friendships and media habits. Avoid a double standard that forbids children to watch impure TV programs but allows adults to do so.

5. Protect your children. Would you pile pornographic magazines in your son's bedroom closet, telling him, "We trust you not to look at them"? This is what you do when you allow him a computer with Internet access in his bedroom.

6. Screen children's clothing. Men are responsible for warning wives and daughters about the dangerous messages that can be conveyed through clothing. Women, please believe us: when we say that a prom dress, shorts, a top, or a swimsuit is inappropriate, we know exactly what we're talking about.

7. Educate children about sex. Every child receives a sex education. The only questions are when, where, and from whom. Parents should be the definitive sex educators.

Teach your children the Purity Principle. Have them write it down and keep it in a place where they can see it often.

If you don't know all the facts, don't be embarrassed. Learn them from Bible-based books. Speak of sex not just as biology but in the context of values, responsibility, and marriage. Teach abstinence as the only biblical option.[1]

8. Know your children—what they are ready for and what they aren't. Honestly answer all questions in an age-appropriate way. Tell your kids as much as they need to know now— not less and not more.

9. Don't procrastinate. Your children's welfare is at stake. Don't wait to have your first talk about sex with your pregnant 15-year-old.

10. Be positive. Discuss the goodness of sex within marriage. Don't be ashamed to talk about what God wasn't ashamed to create.

11. If anyone else is teaching your children about sex, find out exactly what is being said.
12. As with all behavior, teach and model modesty in the home. If your children don't learn modesty from you, they will learn immodesty elsewhere.

Discuss the 12 guidelines with your spouse and agree on the steps you need to initiate with your children. Pray about this subject and decide how you will implement your plans.

THE DAY IN REVIEW

Review today's lesson.
What was the most important concept you read today?

_____

How will this truth challenge you to be like Christ?

_____

_____

Is there a sexual sin you need to confess? If so, confess your sin to God and to your spouse. Repent and receive God's forgiveness and grace. Ask Him also to help you teach your children the biblical ideal of purity. Write your prayer below.

_____

_____

_____

_____

_____

_____

---

[1]True Love Waits is an international campaign that challenges students to commit to remain sexually abstinent until marriage. For information visit *www.truelovewaits.com;* call (800) LUV-WAIT; or write to True Love Waits; One LifeWay Plaza; Nashville, TN 37234-0174.

Accountability and Commitment

Left alone, you cannot win the battle to live a pure life. Use the buddy system to remain accountable. Have someone you can call day or night for help and prayer.

day 5

Let me suggest some guidelines to help keep you accountable.

1. Be active in a local Bible-believing, Christ-centered church:

LET US BE CONCERNED ABOUT ONE ANOTHER IN ORDER TO PROMOTE LOVE AND GOOD WORKS, NOT STAYING AWAY FROM OUR MEETINGS, AS SOME HABIT-UALLY DO, BUT ENCOURAGING EACH OTHER, AND ALL THE MORE AS YOU SEE THE DAY DRAWING NEAR. *HEBREWS 10:24-25*

How can other believers help you, according to these verses?
_____

How can you help other believers? _____
_____

What church are you an active member of? _____

2. Surround yourself with friends who raise the moral bar, not lower it. This verse says it all:

DO NOT BE DECEIVED: BAD COMPANY CORRUPTS GOOD MORALS. *1 CORINTHIANS 15:33*

Think about your friends. Identify anyone who is influencing you to compromise your efforts to be pure. Resolve to discontinue this relationship.

3. Ask a mature Christian to mentor you as you walk in purity.

**If you feel that you need a mentor, name someone
you would like to mentor you.** _____

**If you would like to mentor someone else, name a person
you would like to mentor.** _____

4. Join or form an accountability group. At each meeting,
   each person should answer these key questions:
   • How are you doing with God? With your mate?
     With your children?
   • What temptations are you facing, and how are you
     dealing with them?
   • How has your thought life been this week?
   • Have you spent regular time in the Word and in prayer?
   • With whom have you shared the gospel?
   • Have you lied in any of your answers?
   • How can we pray for you and help you?

Everyone needs accountability—me, you, your pastor, your
spouse, and your kids. One evening I was experiencing strong
sexual temptation that wouldn't cease. Finally I called a brother
I was to have breakfast with the next morning and said, "Please
pray for me and promise to ask me tomorrow morning what I
did." He agreed. The moment I put down the phone, the temptation was gone. Why? I'd like to say it was because I'm so spiritual.
The truth is, there was no way I was going to face this guy the
next morning and have to tell him I had sinned.

My friend was my 911 call. How much better to get imme-
diate help, which prevents sin, rather than report to my group
next week, "I blew it." Honesty about our sin is good—but
honesty about our temptation is even better.

List your 911 friends. If you can't name anyone, find someone!

_____

Those who have gotten help for sexual addictions know that
they must lean on others who are committed to purity. This
battle isn't won alone. When an addict, in bondage to sin,

admits, "I am powerless to change," he can then lean on others outside himself—God above all but also comrades in the fight.

As I look at myself and my brothers and sisters in Christ, I'm deeply concerned about how careless and morally soft we've become. At times we are frighteningly weak in our exercise of sexual purity. We watch and are amused by what offends Holy God. Our tolerance for impurity keeps expanding. Sin sneaks in under our radar. We make ourselves defenseless.

It's time to take a close look at our minds, words, and actions. Think honestly and carefully. Is susceptibility a chink in your armor? If so, following the guidelines in this study may save your life and your family from ruin. It may keep you from forfeiting God's blessings for your future.

If you have already fallen to sexual sin, realize that God has a wonderful promise of hope for you:

IF WE CONFESS OUR SINS, HE IS FAITHFUL AND RIGHTEOUS TO FORGIVE US OUR SINS AND TO CLEANSE US FROM ALL UNRIGHTEOUSNESS.
1 JOHN 1:9

If there is a sin you haven't confessed, stop now, confess it, and receive God's forgiveness.

After confessing your sin, remove the temptation and make changes to ensure that you will not fall again. Forgiveness doesn't mean that you won't experience residual effects of past sins, but it means that you can stop the damage today and enjoy the blessings of purity from now on. God is sovereign and gracious. No matter what we've done, the moment we repent and embrace His forgiveness, we can be in the center of His will. He will demonstrate His amazing grace to us in ways that will delight us. God can cleanse us and make us holy vessels, useful to Himself. Trust God that in time you will reap vast rewards for the purity and faith you exercise today:

WHATEVER GOOD EACH ONE DOES, SLAVE OR FREE, HE WILL RECEIVE THIS
BACK FROM THE LORD. *EPHESIANS 6:8*

I mentioned in day 1 that we would return to very personal
questions. It's time to examine yourself and assess your commitment to sexual purity. Be honest with yourself and take time to
write your answers to these important questions.

How sold out are you to the battle for purity?
What will you do to be sexually pure?

_____

_____

How desperate are you to have victory over sin?
How will you become an overcomer?

_____

_____

How radical are you willing to get for your Lord?
What steps will you take?

_____

_____

_____

How much do you want the joy and peace
that can be found only in God?
What will you do—or not do—to live in His joy and peace?

_____

_____

If we walk daily with Christ, guarding our hearts, depending
on His power, and letting Him transform us through His Word,
then—and only then—can we go our way safely and not be afraid.
Live in such a way as to hear your Lord say to you one day,

WELL DONE, GOOD AND FAITHFUL SERVANT! *MATTHEW 25:21, NIV*

When we hear Him say those incredible words, we will know that any sacrifice we made was nothing.

Record the Purity Principle one last time.

_____

Honor God by living in sexual purity. You'll experience His blessings and rewards not only today, tomorrow, and 10 years from now but also throughout eternity.

THE DAY IN REVIEW

Review today's lesson.
What was the most important concept you read today?

_____

_____

How will this truth challenge you to be like Christ?

_____

_____

Pray about seeking a mentor, being a mentor, or enlisting individuals or joining a group to hold you accountable.
Read the answers you wrote on page 92.
Ask God to help you honor Him through these commitments to sexual purity. Write your prayer below.

_____

_____

_____

_____

_____

Leader Guide

This leader guide provides suggestions for leading a small-group study of *The Purity Principle*. Following this brief introduction, you will find step-by-step guidance for conducting each group session.

Learning Goals

After completing this study, members should be able to—
- define *sexual purity;*
- state the Purity Principle;
- identify the consequences of impurity and the blessings of purity;
- state six biblical strategies for fighting sexual temptation;
- identify guidelines for living a life of purity;
- make a commitment to sexual purity.

Resources

Order in advance one copy of *The Purity Principle* (item 1-4158-2014-7) for each participant. To order, write to LifeWay Church Resources Customer Service; One LifeWay Plaza; Nashville, TN 37234-0113; fax (615) 251-5933; phone toll free (800) 458-2772; e-mail *customerservice@lifeway.com;* order online at *www.lifeway.com;* or visit a LifeWay Christian Store.

If couples are participating, stress that each person should have a copy of the workbook so that he or she can record individual responses to the learning activities.

Group Sessions

Plan for each session to last about an hour. Suggestions are provided to start discussion and to help participants review what they have studied during the week. More activities are provided than you will have time to use, so choose those that will best meet the needs of your group.

Study Options

Although this book contains four weeks of individual study,
you and your group can choose between a four- and five-session
group study.

Four-week plan. Omit the introductory session that follows
and begin with session 1. If you choose this plan, you will
need to give members their workbooks one week before the
study begins so that they can complete their work in week 1
in advance of the first group session.

Five-week plan. The five-week plan begins with the
following introductory session. If you choose this plan, you
can wait until the introductory session to distribute workbooks
because members do not need to prepare for this session.

Introductory Session

Learning Goals

After this session members will be able to—
- identify the goals of this course;
- identify the topics they will study in this course;
- summarize the study format of their workbooks.

Before the Session

1. Provide pens and name tags for participants. Place these on a table near the entrance to the meeting room. Make a name tag for yourself in advance.
2. Have workbooks available for distribution. Place them on the table with the name tags and pens.
3. Familiarize yourself with the content of the study by reading all four weeks.

During the Session

1. As participants arrive, introduce yourself and direct them to the name tags. Also have them pick up their workbooks.
2. After everyone has arrived, welcome the group. State that you look forward to the next four weeks of study, discussion, and fellowship.
3. Ask members to introduce themselves by stating their names and something unique about themselves. Use this time to help participants who might be uncomfortable speaking in front of others to feel more at ease. Limit this activity to 15 minutes.
4. Explain that the subject matter of this study is sensitive but very important. Ask each member to identify whether he or she is married or single and to give his or her expectations of this course. Ask, What motivated you to take this course?
5. State that this study will teach members the biblical meaning of *purity* and God's expectations for a life of purity. Present the learning goals for this course that are listed on page 94.

6. Ask members to open their workbooks to the contents page (p. 3) and have someone read the title of each week's study. Briefly preview each topic.

7. Have members turn to week 1 (p. 6). Explain that each week's material is divided into five days of study. Each day's study includes biblical content, commentary, and learning activities. Tell members to complete each week's study before the related group session. State that the study uses an interactive format. Encourage members to complete the learning activities as they study in order to delve into the Scriptures and to apply the material to their lives. Encourage members to complete one day's material at a time to get the most from their study. State that the weekly group sessions will provide opportunities for review and interaction.

8. Ask members to complete week 1 in their workbooks before the next group session. Instruct them to be ready to discuss the information they study in week 1 during next week's session. State that if they have questions while they are studying, they should write them in the margins of their books and ask them during the group session.

9. Close with a prayer praising God for His lordship over our lives. Ask Him to teach us the biblical meaning of *purity* and biblical guidelines for a life of purity that pleases Him.

Session 1

God's Plan for Sexual Purity

Learning Goals

After this session members will be able to—

- define *sexual purity;*
- state the Purity Principle;
- name three motivations for honoring God's standards for purity;
- state why impurity is idolatry;
- list consequences of impurity;
- explain why the choice between purity and impurity is a life-or-death issue.

Before the Session

1. Provide markers and name tags. Be sure to wear your name tag as people arrive.
2. Study and complete the activities in week 1.
3. Prepare a placard with the definition of *sexual purity* from day 1: *Sexual purity is an absolute commitment of your sexual needs, desires, thoughts, and actions to God.*
4. Prepare Scripture slips with one of the following references on each slip: *Exodus 20:14; Acts 15:20; 1 Corinthians 6:18; Colossians 3:5; 1 Thessalonians 4:7; 1 Timothy 5:22.*
5. Prepare a placard with the Purity Principle: *Purity is always smart; impurity is always stupid.*
6. You will have more activities than you can finish in an hour. Choose the activities that you feel best convey the key concepts in week 1 and best meet the needs of your group.

During the Session

1. Welcome everyone. Begin with prayer, asking God to bless your study and sharing together.
2. Ask a volunteer to tell Lucinda's story in day 1. Ask members

to identify the blessings Lucinda forfeited by choosing impurity. List these on a dry-erase board or chalkboard.

3. Have members suggest definitions of *sexual purity*. Write these definitions on a dry-erase board or chalkboard. Display the placard you prepared with the definition of *sexual purity* and ask members to write it down for reference during the study. Ask members to state the implications of this definition for married and single people (p. 7).

4. State, God commands purity and forbids impurity. Distribute the Scripture slips you prepared and ask members to find and read the Scriptures. As the Scriptures are read, briefly summarize the teachings on purity.

5. Display the placard with the Purity Principle. Ask members to read it together. Point out that there are no exceptions to this principle and that the remainder of this study will provide biblical evidence of its truth.

6. Ask a volunteer to summarize the story of Tiffany and Kyle at the beginning of day 2. State that this kind of misery results when we do not follow God's ideal for purity. Summarize the teachings on God's holiness and emphasize His expectation that we be holy.

7. Divide members into three groups and ask them to summarize from day 2 the three motivations for honoring God's standards for purity: love (pp. 11–12), fear (pp. 12–13), and rewards (pp. 13–14). After group work, call for reports. Summarize that God's design for purity leads to joy.

8. Ask a member to read Jonah 2:8. Ask members to define *idol*. Write responses on a dry-erase board or chalkboard. Ask, How is sexual sin identified as idolatry? (It puts our desires in the place of God.)

9. Have a member read Romans 1:22-32. Ask, What did the people substitute for a relationship with God? List responses on a dry-erase board or chalkboard.

10. Ask members to find evidence in Romans 1:22-32 that Paul was addressing believers. Ask, What do people today

substitute for a relationship with God? Write responses
beside the list in step 9. State that both lists represent
idolatry. Point to the placard with the Purity Principle and
summarize by emphasizing the absurdity of choosing a
material object, a wrong behavior, or a harmful relationship
over the blessing of honoring God.

11. Ask a volunteer to tell Eric's story at the beginning of
day 4. Explain that God has built consequences into the
universe, so wrong choices bring their own punishment.
Ask: What were the consequences of Eric's actions? What
are other possible consequences of impure choices? List all
responses on a dry-erase board or chalkboard.

12. Ask a member to read Matthew 7:24-27. Ask, Why were
the outcomes different for these two men?

13. State, We can be thankful that God's Word teaches us
the consequences of impure choices. Read Proverbs 5:23;
7:22-23. Ask, Why is the choice between purity and
impurity a life-or-death issue? (The ultimate consequence
of immoral behavior is death.)

14. Ask: Did Lucinda, Tiffany, Kyle, and Eric think they were
acting in their best interest? Who deceived them to think
this way? State, Wisdom lies in realizing that when we
follow God's law, we always act in our own interest.

15. Ask a member to read Deuteronomy 30:19-20. State:
To choose purity is to put yourself under God's blessing.
To choose impurity is to put yourself under God's curse.

16. Ask members to read the daily assignments and to complete
the activities in week 2 before the next group session.

17. Close with a prayer thanking God for giving commands
that lead us in the path of purity and joy. Ask Him to
use this study to lead members to choose a life of purity.

Session 2
What's the Big Deal About Sex?

Learning Goals
After this session members will be able to—
- state God's plan for sex;
- describe the destructive power of sex outside marriage;
- identify guardrails for staying within God's boundaries;
- describe Satan's attack on our bodies;
- explain why sexual sin is always exposed;
- distinguish between Satan's voice of deception and God's voice of blessing when facing sexual decisions.

Before the Session
1. Provide markers and name tags. Be sure to wear your name tag as people arrive.
2. Study and complete the activities in week 2.
3. Make three placards with these guardrails for staying within God's boundaries for sex: *Avoid sexual immorality. Learn to control your own body. Don't live in passionate lust.*
4. You will have more activities than you can finish in an hour. Choose the activities that you feel best convey the key concepts in week 2 and best meet the needs of your group.

During the Session
1. Welcome everyone. Begin with prayer, asking God to bless your study and sharing together.
2. Read 1 Corinthians 6:18. Ask, What makes sexual sin different from other sin? (Sex is not just something you do but someone you are; issues of purity cut to the core of who you are and who you will become.)
3. State, Even though sex has the potential for tremendous destructive power, God made it as part of His good creation. Ask a member to read Genesis 1:27. State,

We were created male and female in God's image. Ask a member to read Genesis 1:28. Ask the group to identify the responsibilities of the first man and woman. Ask, What, then, is God's plan for sex? (For a married man and woman to be fruitful, multiply, and fill the earth)

4. Say, Like a fire out of control, sex outside the boundaries God has established brings ruin. Ask members to name devastating and painful effects of sex outside marriage as you list them on a dry-erase board or chalkboard.

5. Ask, What reasons do people give for having sex outside marriage (p. 30)? State: Our feelings and desires do not make it all right to have sex. Only God's boundaries of marriage make sex permissible. Let's look at some guardrails He has established to keep us within His boundaries.

6. Ask a member to read 1 Thessalonians 4:3-8. Display the placard with the guardrail *Avoid sexual immorality.* State that this is clearly God's will, and He expects us to obey.

7. Display the placard with the guardrail *Learn to control your own body.* Read 1 Corinthians 9:25-27 and ask, How do you learn to control your body? (Discipline) Ask members to name ways they can develop discipline for a life of sexual purity. Record these on a dry-erase board or chalkboard.

8. Display the placard with the guardrail *Don't live in passionate lust.* Ask, What is the difference between passion and lust? (Passion is a strong emotion; lust is unbridled sexual desire.) Explain: It's OK and desirable to be passionate about wholesome things, including the pursuit of a vibrant relationship with God. We should love and serve Him passionately.

9. Ask a member to read 1 Corinthians 6:19-20. Ask: To whom do you belong? (God) What was the price of our purchase? (Christ's death on the cross) What is our obligation in regard to our bodies? (Glorify God in our bodies) What is Satan's reaction to the fact that we belong to Christ? (Targets us for attack) State: Satan would like to destroy us, and sexual immorality is one of his weapons.

Therefore, we are foolish if we don't take precautions.
Ask members to name precautions we can take to remain
pure (p. 36). Read 1 Corinthians 10:12.

10. Ask two members to read Proverbs 10:9 and Luke 12:2-3.
Ask, Why is sexual sin always exposed? (God already knows,
and in time others will know.) Using David's example on
pages 40–41, emphasize that we reap what we sow and that
we are always accountable to God.

11. Ask a member to read Cindy's story on page 42. Have
another member read Exodus 20:5. Ask members to name
consequences reaped when we choose sexual immorality.
List these on a dry-erase board or chalkboard. Point out
that these consequences often extend to several generations.
Lead members to quote together the Purity Principle.

12. Read Galatians 6:9. Ask, What ultimate harvest is assured
if we remain faithful in doing good? (A life that pleases
God and the reward of His blessings for all eternity)

13. State, When we face sexual decisions, we must distinguish
between Satan's voice of deception and God's voice of
blessing. Point out Satan's deception in Genesis 3:4-5 and
state that He uses the same tactics today. Ask members to
identify lies Satan whispers when we are sexually tempted.
Ask, What equips you to counter Satan's lies? (God's Word)

14. State, God offers enduring blessings, not cheap thrills. Ask
members to identify some of these blessings by reading the
verses on page 46.

15. Discuss John Piper's statement on pages 46–47. Challenge
members to pursue such a close relationship with God that
they recognize His voice and run to Him when tempted.

16. Ask members to read the daily assignments and to complete
the activities in week 3 before the next group session.

17. Close with a prayer that God will help members live within
His boundaries for sex and withstand Satan's attacks as they
choose God's eternal blessings over temporary pleasures.

Session 3

The Great Temptation

Learning Goals

After this session members will be able to—

- explain why the battle for sexual purity is in the mind;
- name scriptural ways to guard their hearts;
- state six biblical strategies for fighting sexual temptation.

Before the Session

1. Provide markers and name tags. Be sure to wear your name tag as people arrive.
2. Study and complete the activities in week 3.
3. Provide two large sheets of paper and markers for group work.
4. Prepare six placards with the following principles.

    1. Run.

    2. Keep your distance.

    3. Anticipate and prevent temptation.

    4. Cultivate your inner spiritual life.

    5. Memorize and quote Scripture.

    6. Don't give up.

5. You will have more activities than you can finish in an hour. Choose the activities that you feel best convey the key concepts in week 3 and best meet the needs of your group.

During the Session

1. Welcome everyone. Begin with prayer, asking God to bless your study and sharing together.
2. Ask a volunteer to tell Brad's story at the beginning of day 1. Ask members to name the steps that led to Brad's fall. Lead members to quote together the Purity Principle.
3. Ask two members to read Matthew 5:27-28; 15:19 and to identify the source of sin—the heart. Explain that lust feeds on what we have deposited in our brains through our senses.

4. Divide members into two groups and give each group a large sheet of paper and a marker. Ask one group to list harmful deposits we can make in our brains and the other group to list beneficial deposits. After group work, call for reports.

5. Ask, What does the author mean by the statement "Your most important sex organ is your brain" (p. 50)? (Lust, which takes place in the mind, feeds on what the mind takes in.)

6. Discuss the way impure thoughts poison the mind (pp. 50–51). Ask a member to read Ephesians 5:18. Then have the member reread the verse, substituting "don't dwell on lustful things" for "don't get drunk with wine." State, By being continually filled with the Holy Spirit, we choose to replace destructive thoughts with something beneficial.

7. Read Proverbs 4:23 and explain that we guard our hearts by making different choices and changing our habits. State that setting boundaries is one way we guard our hearts. Ask members to name boundaries that can protect sexual purity.

8. State, Scripture teaches us how to store good thoughts in our minds and reject evil ones. Ask three members to read the following Scriptures: Romans 12:2; Colossians 3:2; and Colossians 3:5. After each verse is read, ask the group to identify what we should reject and what we should do. Record responses on a dry-erase board or chalkboard.

9. Say, Let's look at six biblical principles for overcoming sexual temptation. Display the first of the six placards you prepared as a member reads 1 Corinthians 6:18. State the first principle: *Run.* Briefly remind members of Joseph's example. Ask, How do we run from sexual temptation today?

10. Display the second placard as you introduce the corresponding principle: *Keep your distance.* Explain: The idea isn't to go as far as you can without stepping over the line. The goal is absolute obedience to God's command. If He says something is wrong, our response should be to stay away from it.

11. Display the placard for the third strategy: *Anticipate and*

prevent sexual temptation. Point out the examples on page 61. Assign groups of three to identify and report on steps we can take to anticipate and prevent sexual temptation.

12. Show the fourth placard as you state the strategy: *Cultivate your inner spiritual life.* Explain the difference between behavior modification and spiritual transformation (p. 62). State, The battle for purity is won not through trying harder but only through the indwelling power of the risen Christ. Ask, How can believers cultivate their spiritual lives?

13. Refer to Jesus' temptation by Satan in Matthew 4:2-11. Ask, How did Jesus deal with temptation? (By quoting Scripture He had hidden in His heart) Display the fifth placard as you identify the strategy: *Memorize and quote Scripture.* Ask, What is so strategic about memorizing and quoting Scripture? (If God's Word is stored in our hearts, we are ready to fight when temptation comes.)

14. State the principle on the sixth placard: *Don't give up.* Ask a member to read James 4:7-8. Ask: What are we to do in regard to God? In regard to the Devil? What are the outcomes?

15. State that our resources for resisting temptation are supernatural and powerful. Have three members read 2 Corinthians 5:21; 2 Peter 1:3-4; and Titus 2:11-12. Challenge members to appropriate Christ's righteousness, power, and grace to fight the battle with sexual temptation. Emphasize that because He lives in us, victory is possible.

16. Review the six strategies. Then remove the placards and ask members to write down the strategies from memory. Read the strategies again to check members' memories.

17. Ask members to read the daily assignments and to complete the activities in week 4 before the next group session.

18. Close by praying that God will guide members to guard their hearts and to store up godly thoughts in their minds. Pray that He will empower members to apply these biblical strategies to fight and gain victory over sexual temptation.

Session 4
Getting Personal

Learning Goals

After this session members will be able to—

- explain why radical choices are necessary for sexual purity;
- identify guidelines for living a life of purity;
- identify guidelines for teaching children about sexual purity;
- state the importance of accountability in remaining sexually pure;
- state the requirement for receiving God's forgiveness when they sin;
- make a commitment to sexual purity.

Before the Session

1. Provide markers and name tags. Be sure to wear your name tag as people arrive.
2. Study and complete the activities in week 4.
3. Provide three large sheets of paper and markers for group work.
4. Make a copy of the following commitment for each member.

My Commitment

Through the power of Christ, who lives in me,
I commit my sexual needs, desires, thoughts, and
actions to God, and I resolve to remain sexually pure
in thoughts, words, and actions from this day forward.

Signed _____ Date _____

5. You will have more activities than you can finish in an hour. Choose the activities that you feel best convey the key concepts in week 4 and best meet the needs of your group.

During the Session

1. Welcome everyone. Begin with prayer, asking God to bless your study and sharing together.

2. Ask the group to name sexually immoral behaviors that are depicted on television shows. Write these on a dry-erase board or chalkboard. Ask, What effect does watching these behaviors have on our minds and morals? (They are part of Satan's strategy to normalize evil. They desensitize us and our children to God's hatred of sexual immorality.) Read Proverbs 8:13.

3. Ask a member to read Matthew 5:27-30. Ask: What did Jesus say we should do if our right eye causes us to sin? If our right hand causes us to sin? Explain that Jesus wasn't saying that our eye and our hand actually cause the sin. But the eye is used to access godly and ungodly information. The hand is used to perform righteous or sinful acts. Jesus used a radical image to stress that we must govern what our eyes look at and what our hands do.

4. Call for responses to the activity at the bottom of page 72. Ask, Why are radical choices necessary to sexual purity? (As Jesus illustrated, it's the only way to get serious about rejecting the evil that God hates.) Summarize that no sacrifice is too great for those who want to please their Savior and Lord.

5. Divide members into three groups. Give each group a large sheet of paper and a marker. Assign one group to list and report on the guidelines for single adults' sexual purity in day 2. Assign another group to list and report on the guidelines for couples' sexual purity in day 3. Assign the third group to list and report on the remaining guidelines for couples' sexual purity in day 4. Be prepared to add needed information as the groups report. Also provide an opportunity for members to respond to the guidelines by adding to them or by commenting on any they find helpful. Encourage singles to spend time after the session applying the guidelines to their lives. Encourage couples to plan a time after the session to discuss ways they will assess and implement the guidelines.

6. Ask, Why is accountability so important to sexual purity? (The temptations are strong; we need others' support in order to win the battle for purity; sometimes they are our 911 call to keep us faithful.) Encourage members to be accountable to someone for their sexual purity.

7. Emphasize the importance of confession of our sin when we fall. Ask a member to read 1 John 1:9. Ask: What is the requirement? What has God promised to do? Say: If you have failed in the area of sexual purity, confess your sin and receive God's forgiveness. Then resolve, with God's help, to remain pure from now on. I hope the guidance in this study will help you do that.

8. Ask members to look at their responses to the personal questions on page 92. Challenge them to answer the questions if they have not already done so.

9. Distribute copies of the commitment you prepared and ask members to sign the commitment and to keep it for future reference. Encourage them to use their commitment as a source of accountability.

10. Lead the group to repeat the Purity Principle. Read Proverbs 3:21-26.

11. Close the session by praying that God will give members strength and resolve to follow through with any commitments they have made to live pure lives that please Him.

More discipleship studies by

RANDY ALCORN

Small courses. Big impact.

the GRACE *and* TRUTH PARADOX

Our world today needs both grace and truth. By learning to show these qualities in balance, you can redemptively reflect Jesus' character as you offer others the hope and need for salvation in Him.

ISBN 0-6331-9755-6

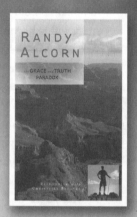

the TREASURE PRINCIPLE

The treasure principle is a simple yet profound idea—with radical implications. When you discover the joy of investing in eternity, you'll never be content with less.

RELEASES APRIL 2005

ISBN 1-4158-2015-5

Order online at www.lifeway.com or call 1-800-458-2772.